Marijuana
Daily Gardening

How to Grow

Indoors Under

Fluorescent

Lights

T0161451

Henry Woodward

Green Candy Press

Copyright © 2015 Henry Woodward
Published by Leahbar Inc.
Toronto, Canada

ISBN 978-1937866-26-6

Images © Henry Woodward

Printed in China by Everbest Printing Co. through Four Colour Print Group.

Sometimes Massively Distributed by P.G.W.

For two late greats: Gerhardt and Doug.

Contents

Getting Started

Congratulations! Welcome to the "growing" community of home marijuana cultivators. The decision to start a home garden can be a difficult one. Well, actually, compared to what can be a bewildering number of considerations in setting up your daily grow for the first time, the decision itself can be comparatively easy. However, my new grower friends should have no fear: the path from complete newbie to experienced cannabis gardener is short, interesting, and definitely rewarding.

I am writing this book as a gardener of moderate experience, specifically for would-be growers with little or no experience. You might be asking why on Earth you should be trusting anyone who is less than a pro. Well, as much as I appreciate the advice of professional growers and have learned from some of their books, I think there are several reasons that a more grassroots book will help new growers. The first is that professional growers are engaged in a number of sophisticated processes (for instance, creating new strains through breeding) and techniques (such as using sophisticated control boards to manage advanced lighting, hydroponic systems and release carbon dioxide) that need not concern those just starting out, at least until their skills and knowledge are well established.

The second is that pro grows are very different animals: big, expensive, and potentially very risky (especially if pursued in jurisdictions where it is criminalized by high-minded but wrong-headed moralism). Your home garden likely cannot and surely need not be any of these things. Though a daily grow can be challenging at times, it is more simple than you might think while reading this introduction and weighing how to approach your own garden. The perspective of someone not too far removed from their own first-timer questions (and who from time-to-time still make mistakes, as you no doubt will) is invaluable for someone, like yourself, who will face just similar situations.

Finally, unlike many professionals, I don't have a huge ego regarding my reputation as a grower. Many writers and even amateur bloggers can be reluctant to share their mistakes. Not so here. This grow will illustrate not only the successes but also the failures and even the completely embarrassing screw-ups that we all make. This grow journal will show the good, the bad and, yes, even the ugly (and there have been some real ugly mistakes, let me tell you). With any luck, it will help you to maximize your chances of achieving the first and avoiding the other two.

We'll be kicking it old school in this grow: (high quality) soil, water, lights, and a nutritious diet for your little ladies. The rest are just details. You'll get them here.

About Me

I began growing nearly five years ago. At the time, I was not even a regular cannabis smoker beyond the occasional toke at a party, let alone a daily vaporizer as I am today. I had never seen a cannabis plant first hand, let alone grown one myself. My personal knowledge of marijuana was limited to what I had picked up in popular culture and, as such, was fairly limited and marked by the stereotype of the slacker-stoner, head shops, and hydroponic supply ads. That is to say, I was a complete and total beginner.

Though I have pretty standard outdoor gardens on my home property, I didn't by any stretch consider myself a green thumb – in fact, houseplants have not enjoyed a track record of success in my home.

Since I have a day job as a university professor, I enjoy learning and teaching, and quickly found a passion for cannabis cultivation. Needless to say though, I didn't fit the normal profile of a typical grower/user. That was the first part of my own education: in my view today, these stereotypes have been perpetuated by powerful voices in government, law enforcement, and the alcohol lobby to keep the general public ignorant of how benign, enjoyable, and healing marijuana can be. Today, I count myself as someone who strongly believes that the distinction between "medical" and "recreational" pot is an artificial distinction. Marijuana is a plant. It comes from nature. Used responsibly, it is safe, effective, and easy to enjoy.

So what motivated me to start growing? Equal parts chance and a health emergency experienced by a close family member. Several years ago, my partner was diagnosed with epilepsy. Marijuana was prescribed to mitigate the effect of seizures she experienced multiple times daily. She continues to use it daily in conjunction with pharmaceuticals to keep seizures at bay, which they thankfully have been for some time. Indeed, the anti-convulsive effects of cannabis are well if incompletely documented, and my partner has been advised by medical doctors to continue her daily prescribed use of marijuana to maintain her health. But confronted with a need to secure a regular supply of high quality cannabis, we needed to find a source.

At first, my partner sought out what is for many people the only source of marijuana: illegal drug dealers. Though the cost was high, supply was at least regular. But though I know many people maintain contacts to secure pot with people who are dependable and trustworthy, we worried that the handful of sources that we had were potentially dangerous, and not a little unsavory. As a woman walking into places without escort, often in the company of numerous unknown men, she (and I) began to worry about her safety. Here is a genuine danger associated with marijuana use, but to be clear, it is one created by the current legal regime in most places, not the plant itself. There had to be a better way. We began investigating.

From here, we quickly dismissed government-produced cannabis. I'm a believer in the idea that government can be a force for good in our society. But they sure do produce crappy pot. The sealed bags sent from the government were both expensive and of poor quality: it was clear that entire plants were ground up together, not just the bud that is high in THC or CBD, but also much lower impact stems and leaves. Strains were not advertised, it was just generic "pot," and overly dry and poorly cured at that. This, coupled with the resistance and often outright refusal (until very recently) of either government or health care professionals to fund and conduct controlled experiments on the efficacy of marijuana consumption for different physical and psychological ailments, meant that we were powerless to identify strains that might best address the symptoms of the medical license holder. The pot bought from the government was a poor deal in terms of quality. It made illegally-sourced pot a superior option. Coupled with punitive laws for possession of marijuana, we had hit strike two in our search for a good source.

We then located several good sources of quality weed via compassion clubs that only accepted clients with valid government permits to possess cannabis for medical use. This made buying pot more (but not totally) safe and secure, and the price was similar: some strains were cheaper than what was available illegally; other more sought-after strains were more expensive. It also meant that we could purchase edibles in some cases, with a reasonable if not total safety guarantee. Still, these sources currently exist in a legal gray area. We worried about the continued potential for having to deal with law enforcement. The monthly purchase of pot continued to be a hassle, potentially at risk in terms of purchase and transport (who likes walking around with hundreds of dollars worth of cannabis or money to buy cannabis on their person between a store and home if they can avoid it?) and still very expensive.

It was at this point that we made the decision to start a home grow. By necessity, as a result of the severity of my partner's medical condition at the time, responsibility for this start up fell to me.

I began documenting the work for this book in my garden's first year, in large part because I knew so little and was committed to improving my grow techniques and the quantity and quality of the product in successive harvests. I took extensive notes, and experimented with what worked and what didn't. I asked questions at my local hydroponics and head shops when people agreed to share their experiences. Failing this, I researched online and via existing grow books when I had questions I couldn't answer. Slowly, my garden took shape and improved.

Though there is a wealth of knowledge out there to access once you know where to look, it struck me that there was no book that I could find that could speak explicitly to my experience as a newbie marijuana cultivator. Most books were written by pros, for pros. Others, even explicitly written for beginners, tended to show grows that were perfect or at least without major incidents. This makes sense: for most people in the industry, there is a fair amount of pride (and ego) that accompanies an established practice. What I needed was a book that wouldn't hide the many errors and pitfalls of an initial grow. A book that would share simple, cost-effective solutions to common problems. A book that was written for a beginner, by a beginner. I decided that I would write that book. You're holding the results of that effort. It follows one of my earliest grows, at a time when I was just learning my craft. I haven't airbrushed mistakes I made. I wrote the book I wish I had had when I was starting. I hope it will help fill this need for you.

Before moving on, I must note that becoming an amateur home gardener has been a profoundly positive experience for my family and for me. We now have a source of cannabis that is secure. It costs literally pennies on the dollar compared to what we used to pay others, even after setup and annual expenses. We control the genetics. We control the grow conditions, which is important for the health conscious: we don't have to worry about buying pot that has been sprayed with poisonous insecticides, or laced with anything else we wouldn't choose to consume. We have the ability to manipulate relative THC/CBD levels based on when we harvest (this takes a lot of trial and error, but it is an unbelievably interesting and rewarding process). Moreover, we have been able to locate and produce a dependable source of strains that best impact the health needs of the primary user for whom I am growing. By taking control of our own medicine, we have taken control of our own health.

Finally, I would be remiss not to admit that I now enjoy marijuana on a daily basis. It has improved my mood, been a trusted pain reliever and anti-inflammatory, and a healthier option for altering my mental state than consuming mass units of alcohol (and yes, while the "munchies" are real for me as they are for many cannabis users, I have dropped twenty pounds as pot has largely replaced fattening beer as part of my daily routine). I hadn't really intended to use cannabis much if at all, even when I had started growing. But it is a poor cook or vintner who doesn't try his or her own product, no? There has also been an additional mental health benefit to growing that I have rarely seen mentioned: growing cannabis in your home with proper preparation is generally safe, easy, and inexpensive. But it is also deeply relaxing and even therapeutic. The time I spend in my garden most days is one of the most quiet and relaxing parts of my day. I genuinely derive a benefit from spending time with my plants, which I care for and about a great deal. You might be pleasantly surprised to find that this will happen to you as well.

But that isn't to suggest that establishing and operating a home grow isn't a significant amount of work. With that in mind, let's turn our attention to the grow itself.

My Home Grow

In terms of layout, I use a fairly compact grow space. The room is located in a small closet-like room in an unfinished basement. The basement itself is only about five feet high at its highest points which puts vertical height at a premium – I have to grow smartly and with good planning to ensure that my grow stays within the confines of my work space; particularly height-inclined sativas.

The entire grow room is lined by white polyethylene tarp to add to the reflectivity of the space. It is four feet wide and just over four feet high (though the ceiling is unfinished, so there is a bit of play there). It is ten feet long, divided into three roughly equally-sized chambers by polyethylene tarps secured by Velcro that allow each room to be easily accessed while remaining light-tight at all other times. The central area provides a small work area in the middle, which houses the power bars and other electrical equipment. The bud and vegetation rooms are accessed on each side via the tarps, and the whole set up is secured behind a locking door. It is as inconspicuous as possible from the outside and the area just outside of the grow rooms can be quickly tidied to remove most evidence that anything unusual is going on, in case someone such as a service worker must access the basement. In short, it is utilitarian: easy to clean, organized, and secure, with all necessary tools in easy reach.

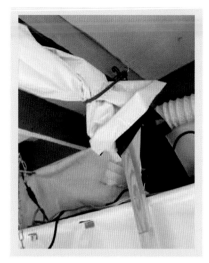 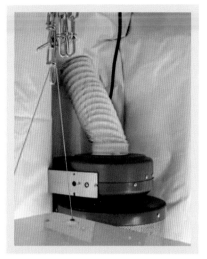

Hang polyethylene tarps cut to fit your grow space. They are a snap to clean and can be quickly rolled up and secured with Bungee cords, and can be made flat with Velcro at the edges so that no light escapes.

Measure your grow space before purchasing an exhaust fan. Be sure to purchase one that will evacuate warm air frequently.

The walls and floor are concrete, which makes for a clean and cleanable workspace. However, it means that the plants must be raised ever so slightly off the floor so that roots won't be too cold. Moreover, the room itself isn't heated or cooled by the house's forced-air system, basements tend to be cooler than the rest of the house in the summer. At times, this can make it difficult to keep the rooms in an optimum temperature range. This is one advantage of using T5 fluorescents: they don't kick a lot of extra heat into an already hot space.

To keep plants from being placed directly on concrete, the rooms have a plywood floor in the veg room (painted and sealed to make for easier clean up) and rubber "play mats" (what kids in a kindergarten would use in a playroom to reduce fall injuries) in the bud room. These are superior to raised shelves because both the plywood and mats use less than an inch of the precious grow space on the vertical axis. Shelves to hold the plants would use up too much space to allow for a good grow with only four feet of play.

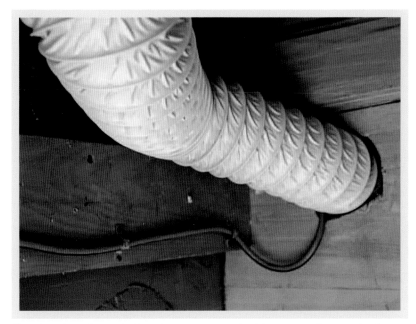

Simple tubing for a clothes dryer vent can double as an exhaust tube for your grow space.

Oscillating fans are set up in each grow room, also just off the floor to avoid issues in case of spills. An exhaust fan with a carbon filter sits on a shelf near the ceiling of the bud room – a must since it must filter and evacuate air that carries telltale odors when plants are near harvest. All wires are secured to walls using clips that are nailed into studs – it is literally impossible that wires will fall into water. Ventilation tubes have been constructed (out of standard exhaust tubes used for a clothes dryer) and placed behind the polyethylene on the walls to encourage airflow into and out of the room. These are curved to ensure that rooms remain light-tight: that is, no ambient light from outside the grow rooms can enter via vent access points.

For lighting, a band of T5 fluorescents, each a foot wide and four feet long that house four 54 watt T5 tubes apiece, are hung from chains to allow lights to be easily moved up and down as plants grow. The chains are in turn secured to ceiling studs – the lights are very secure and won't fall or be easily disturbed. The work areas are also fitted with green incandescent bulbs. This allows work to be done in dark periods

Lights should be hung from chains to allow for easy movement up and down. Secure chains to hooks that will safely bear the weight of your setup.

where the T5s are off and the plants are resting. The green bulbs access a part of the light spectrum that won't disturb the plants. This is a must for any grower.

Outside of the grow rooms is a work area that doubles as a normal basement workshop. The tools and equipment help hide the true nature of this area's primary use. All grow supplies are kept in secure shelves that can be cleaned up in less than five minutes. A separate closet nearby (measuring four square feet) is used for drying and curing bud, as well as storage of other supplies such as mason jars (for bottling bud), shelving (for raising seedlings closer to the T5s when other, larger plants must also be under the lights), additional nutrients (for feeding), and additional light bulbs as well as other miscellaneous gear.

Beyond this, I have also installed a good set of stereo speakers so that I can easily play music or listen to the ball game on the radio. This might seem like a small detail, but given that even a small grow can be a time consuming hobby, it is important to have such creature comforts ready to go when possible. Cold beer and a vaporizer are also steps

Hot air rises! Raise your exhaust vent and be sure to make the exhaust tube light-tight so that no light from outside can disturb sleeping beauties.

away. As a result, I'm more than happy to spend hours each week in my secret garden.

The only real shortfall of this setup is the lack of easy access to water. There is no sink in the basement and consequently I must lug pails of water downstairs each day. This is something I want to address in the future. If you have a small work sink (as one would typically find in a laundry room) nearby for watering plants and cleaning up, that is a big plus.

Since I began this grow journal with some plants already partially matured, there are two Master Kush females in my home garden as of right now. They are confirmed females since they were grown from previously sexed clones taken from a mother plant. Master Kush is a pure indica strain. Typical of the Kush family, it really packs a punch in terms of effects, but I chose to grow it because it has a relatively "small nose" (i.e. it doesn't stink like some more skunky strains), and has a clean taste when vaporized – just a hint of pine needles and maybe a bit of lemon but the weed itself really shines through.

The grow journal that follows documents the continuation of this strain:

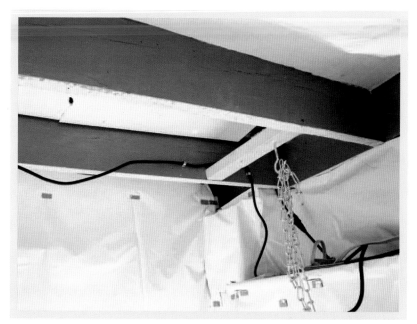

Be sure to secure all wires to make your garden a safe workspace.

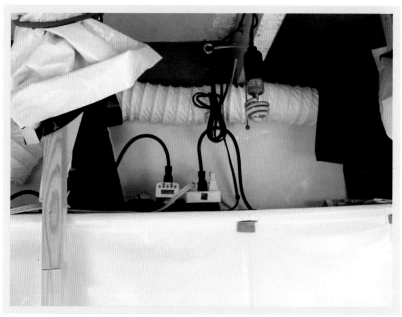

Timers and power bars should be kept off the floor. It is a good idea to label each wire with a nametag. This takes the guesswork out of unplugging lights or other appliances when needed.

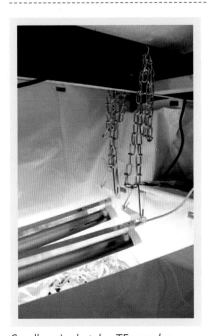

Smaller, single tube T5s can be easily added to compact grow spaces.

I start by taking several new Master Kush clones to propagate the next generation of plants. It also involves the germination of a new strain in my garden: Tangerine Dream, a sativa-dominant hybrid. I am growing these from seed that came billed as a good "daytime smoke" since Tangerine is supposed to taste of citrus and to cultivate a cerebral rather than body high. The idea here is to create a crop of plants that can be alternated for use during the day and at night.

Since this grow, I've graduated to more than a dozen different strains (and counting) as I continue to experiment with new growing methods and new strains. I also like to renew the genetics of each plant strain (starting over from seed) at least once a year, and this allows me to decommission particular strains when I have created an adequate supply and to then move on to new ones or to reintroduce strains of times gone past. With some preparation and a bit of hard work, you can be here too. Let's take a look at how to get you there.

Preparing Your Grow Room

Detail number one is perhaps the most crucial consideration: where to grow? Your first task will be to survey and prepare the location of your grow room or rooms. There isn't really a limit on the size of your grow space, apart from the amount of physical space you have to work with, and what you can easily manage. A grow can also be very compact, sometimes no larger than a moderately sized closet.

Above all, choose a location that is secure. Account for daily use of the space in your home or apartment. Will guests or visitors such as repair people need and be able to access this space? Ideally, the answer to this will be no. Choose a space that is inconspicuous. Your space will also be one that can quickly be swept clear if, for instance, a furnace repair or emergency visit from a plumber is required nearby. It should be a space that can be locked. This is also a consideration for would-be gardeners who have kids. You'll probably want to avoid a conversation with the parents of your child's friend about the strange, stinky garden they found while playing Hide and Go Seek at your house! You should definitely have the ability to lock it down, even if it is something that you rarely, if ever, have to do.

Basements are ideal, particularly those typical of old houses that may be little more than a glorified crawl space, unfinished and largely not subject to much traffic. Attics, which typically lack proper insulation let alone air conditioning, can be too hot in the summer and cold in the winter to use effectively. Spaces in close proximity to a washroom, laundry area or even water tank are also good, provided they can be hidden, because this makes watering your garden less time consuming. Watering plants will be the most time consuming part of your daily grow. You will also have a frequent need to clean up the room, the tools, and even yourself. Hauling water buckets up and down some stairs isn't the end of the world, but it is also not ideal. Choose a space that you will be comfortable working in; you will spend hours over the life of your garden, or even a single grow, in this space. Ask yourself this: would you choose to hang out here, even if nobody else would? Even small touches make a big difference. In my case, I purchased of a good set of speakers to allow me to play music or listen to the radio from my iPhone while working. These things matter. If tending to your garden is a drag, you're more likely to avoid it, give it insufficient attention or otherwise make avoidable mistakes. Make this space a room into your own little haven!

One final consideration: this book details the particulars of indoor grows only. You may have an outdoor space that is ideal for growing, a cottage or farm property with a quiet space or even a fenced and heavily shielded back yard in the city, one that for instance is lush with the growth of many plants that can hide one or more marijuana plants in its leafy confines, and you might understandably be very tempted to start a grow there. However, I strongly discourage such grows. They are definitely

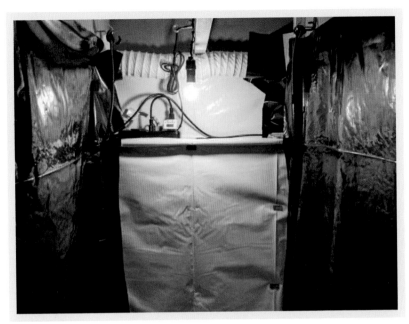

Green lights are a must. They allow cannabis to effectively remain in the dark cycle. This is important for when you need to work in the garden at these times.

much less secure and the chance of discovery by a friend, a would-be thief or, worst of all, a law enforcement agent also grows exponentially in these situations. Outdoor growing of any type, and most especially "guerilla" style grows (ones where you plant one or more cannabis plants surreptitiously in a public space or on property belonging to another person) are definitely not for the faint of heart.

Your chosen grow space will also need to be properly wired. Ensure that you have access to an adequate number of electrical outlets before you start building; my small rooms consistently use no less than seven plugs when lights, fans, vents and, occasionally, space heaters are considered. If you will be using extension cords, they should be secured to reduce the chances of tripping or immersing in spilled water.

Power bars and timers (or best, power bars with timer functionality) are a must to control different light schedules. Finally, do some rough and easy to figure calculations: does your home or apartment have sufficient wattage to meet your needs? Perhaps the only thing worse than an

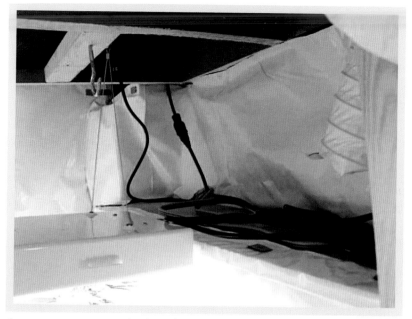

An unnecessary mess: tie down loose wires and cords with Velcro straps or twist ties.

insecure room that is discovered is an improperly wired room that results in a fire. When it comes to safety, don't skimp and don't take chances.

Once the space is selected, you will need to prepare the room (or rooms) properly. Soon, you'll have new baby plants growing here. You definitely want to prep the babies' room before they come home. Ideally, you will have sufficient space to create two dedicated rooms in which you will grow and maintain your garden: a "veg" room and a "bud" room. The veg room will house plants grown from seed or cloned cuttings and will expose them to a light cycle that is either 18/6 light to dark or even has the lights on 24/7. The other room will be the "bud" room, a space into which physically mature plants will be moved when vegging is complete. This room will be set up on a 12/12 light/dark cycle, meant to mimic the shorter days of the autumn harvest season. It is essential that each room is light-tight. Escaping light could arouse suspicion from passersby and light entering could actually harm your grow, particularly light bleeding into a sloppily assembled bud room. A larger room can even be split into two sections with relative ease. This

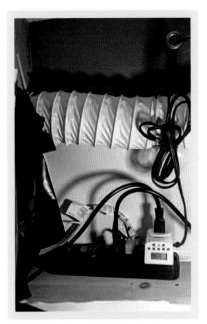

At least two timers are required to operate two rooms on different light cycles. Here a small timer is plugged into a power bar that also has a separate timer.

book shows a grow conducted in a room smaller than a typical walk-in closet that has been split into two rooms; that is, less than four feet tall with each room measuring about four feet across and less than that deep, with a small antechamber of similar size in between the two grow rooms.

If you can dedicate one other small space of say four feet across by two deep and two high, you will also be able to create a dedicated space for hanging your harvested bud to dry. This room is the easiest to assemble: all it really requires is a space where you can string several lengths of string like clothes lines, tied securely and with sufficient clearance (a minimum of 18 inches to be safe) to

Cleaning Your Grow Room

1. Avoid accumulation of dead vegetative matter, particularly in pots as it can breed mould and attract pests.

2. Clean up spills immediately whenever possible.

3. Use vinegar to disinfect all soiled surfaces between grows.

4. Sweep/vacuum regularly.

5. If rodents are present (e.g. if grow room is located in a basement), be sure to set ample traps in the vicinity of the grow.

6. Deal with spider webs. Never allow webs to be set on or near plants.

7. Clean tops of nutrient bottles to seal well after use. Otherwise, gummy remnants will accumulate.

8. Keep buckets used for watering clean. Rinsing should be sufficient day-to-day, but clean occasionally with soap and water (after each grow for instance).

9. Keep work area clean and free of household crap as much as possible so you have an organized work area.

Something way better than clothes will be drying on these lines!

hang stems while they dry. Finally, you will need space to work (a basement work bench is ideal) that is adequately lit and that allows for easy access to stored tools and supplies.

If you are truly challenged in terms of the space you can dedicate to your garden and can only have one room, you will likely want to opt for autoflowering seeds. These will be described in the grow journal below. They are perhaps the best strategy for a daily grow in a truly tiny garden.

Once the space is selected, ensure that you clean the area thoroughly. Avoid the temptation to skip this important step. You want an environment that is as sterile as possible. Sweep and vacuum the area. Remove any dust or cobwebs. Clean all surfaces with vinegar or a diluted bleach solution. Your grow room can be compromised by pests before you even start growing if you neglect a good cleaning. This is something you will want to commit to from time to time in any case. I generally clean my rooms at the end of each grow cycle to stay on top of any problems developing. It might seem tedious, but this is far less work than getting rid of an infestation in the middle of a grow cycle!

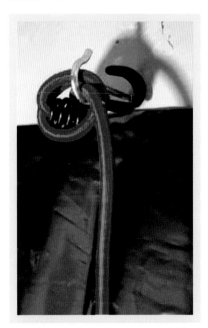 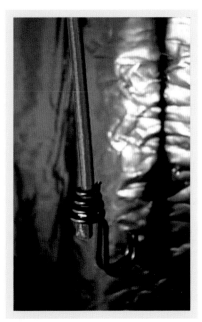

Bungee cords are a cheap and effective way to keep polyurethane barriers secured while you work in your garden. Hang from hooks so they can be used to easily tie back tarps.

After cleaning, your grow space must be prepared by tacking up polyurethane that is white on one side and black on the other. Both rooms should be lined on all sides with this wrap. Ceilings and floors need not be wrapped (ceilings are beyond the lights and floors are too high traffic and will need frequent clean up from small spills of water, dirt and plant material). Polyurethane can be bought relatively inexpensively in rolls at a hydroponic store or even garden center. When purchasing materials, the persona of a home cook interested in cultivating their own herbs year-round is a nice, safe identity to assume to avoid arousing any suspicion.

You may have heard that silver Mylar is best for this lining your walls with, since it is highly reflective, but really, it isn't necessary. The white polyurethane is an excellent light reflector and much sturdier. It is less prone to rip and can be wiped clean with ease, so skip the Mylar. The plastic on these rolls is thick enough that a portion cut to size can be hung as a "wall" in a grow space that has been bisected into two rooms, as mine has. In fact, using polyurethane as a barrier is highly efficient because it can easily be secured and made light-tight with Velcro bought in rolls or tabs. Also, it can easily be rolled, as one would a tarp or tent fly, and secured to the upper extent of a wall or the adjoining ceiling using bungee cords hung from hooks.

When lining your grow room, you will need a staple gun to secure the polyurethane to walls or, in the case of an unfinished space such as a basement, exposed studs. The latter is fine: finished walls are redundant after lining the grow area. One important tip you should consider: to reduce the likelihood of rips, cut up small squares of cardboard to place over the poly when stapling. By stapling through the cardboard, you will secure the plastic in a way that minimizes the chance of a rip if it is tugged or stretched. Replacing polyurethane that has been ripped mid-grow is a time consuming job that is definitely no fun.

Sterilizing Pots and Trays

1. Best to do this semi-frequently so that you minimize "burning" the nutrients onto the trays.

2. Always use disinfected pots and trays to avoid transferring problems like insects or infections from one generation of plants to the next.

3. It is best to clean outside or in a basement – it can be messy. Keep in mind privacy considerations: avoid conspicuous cleaning of numerous pots and tools that may tip off a nosy neighbour.

4. Dispose of used soil, roots, etc. before starting. Do not "recycle" soil, since soil that has been subjected to more than three months of heavy nutrient use can be depleted and can result in "soil-lock". Always start with fresh soil in each grow.

5. Use gloves and work clothes as you will be using bleach.

6. Solution: 9 parts hot water, 1 part bleach (quarts).

7. Use scrub brushes and scouring pads.

8. Let stubborn stains soak. Scrub. Soak again. Repeat.

9. Air dry. Pots must, MUST be allowed to dry fully before use. Otherwise bleach residue could harm plants.

10. Once dry, rinse pots well. Ideally, use a hose to save time and effort when sterilizing many pots. Let them air dry again.

11. Sterilized pots and trays can be returned to the grow room to dry to minimize hassle and security concerns.

12. Remember to sterilize stakes also – they can carry infection too!

A cardboard box cut into little squares is an effective way to ensure that staples don't rip polyethylene sheeting. Use these when constructing your grow room and have extras on hand in case repairs are needed.

Going Shopping

Next, you will need to make two trips: one to a local hardware store, and a second to a local grow or hydroponics shop; these can be found in most medium size cities these days. At the hardware store, you will need to purchase tools necessary for the installation of the lights and setup of timers. You will also need to pick up a number of tools (e.g. shears and at least one set of small, sharp scissors, hooks and chains for hanging lights, etc.) and other odds and ends such as buckets, a plastic measuring cup and spoons and more. If you are on a budget, many of these materials can be located in dollar stores. You definitely will not want to skimp on your hardware (such as lights) or "software" such as seed and nutrients, but you don't exactly need a set of pewter measuring spoons. A bargain bin plastic set will do the job more than adequately. Refer to the photo essay below ("A Grow Room Shopping List") for more details.

At your hydroponics store, you will be able to buy necessary prod-

Security

1. Talk to NO ONE about your new hobby. You will anyway, but don't. You can never take this back. It is normal to want to discuss, even brag about your new project. But resist the urge.

2. Even someone you trust may talk about your grow to others that are less trustworthy.

3. Consider the 24 Hour Rule: when tempted to talk about your garden to someone new, wait for a full day. If it still seems like a good idea at that time, okay. You might be surprised how often a second thought will result in a closed mouth!

4. Garbage disposal: to avoid risk of detection, dispose of anything that might cause suspicion in secured garbage bags. Avoid recycling materials (e.g. seed pods or empty nutrient bottles) if they might be discovered, for instance by someone searching for returnable alcohol bottles in your bins. Opt for the garbage instead.

5. Leaves culled from plants and trim from harvest can be kept in a green bin in your grow room work area. When disposing of vegetative material, be sure to hide this green garbage in food scraps, for instance.

6. Make a habit of conducting weekly checks for smell or any other sign that might advertise your garden. Take steps to address security "leaks" proactively.

7. Soil that has been spent can easily be spread in a home garden if you have access to one. You may want to spread it after dark or as part of regular home gardening (the non-cannabis variety) to avoid attracting suspicion.

ucts that won't be available at either a hardware store or garden center. You might assume, wrongly, as I did when setting up my first garden, that the lighting section of the hardware store would have the bulbs and ballast equipment you need. Wrong. You need to go to the pros for this stuff. Come prepared and read online before going so that you know what you are looking for and can save time, or at least have a better idea of what questions to ask staff. Here, you can buy the nutrients needed for your grow. Go slowly: you don't need to buy every advanced nutrient, additive or gadget. This trip can get expensive quickly, so keep it simple. Your "local" should also stock a variety of plastic pots, trays and the like. They will have dry soil mixes, which are much less likely to be infested with pests than bagged potting soil from the hardware store (another place you definitely don't want to skimp to save a few bucks!).

A Grow Room Shopping List

Tools and Supplies

- You can get a lot of stuff at your local hardware store (but not lights!). You should go to a hydroponic store for "dedicated" grow tools and nutrients, such as these from General Hydroponics:

- Demineralized water
- Spray bottle of water for clones
- Nutrients and nutrient guide
- Measuring cup, water bucket, and spoons
- Seed/clone pods, bubbles, trays, medium (1 gallon)
- Large pots (3 gallon) with holes in base for drainage
- Potting soil
- Newspaper for lining pots (keep in soil/roots)
- Stakes and green garden ties (for maximizing proximity to lights as they grow)

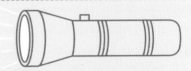

- Lights, such as the T5 fluorescents used in my garden
- Flashlight for checking the garden and electrics in the dark
- Fans for air circulation
- Exhaust fan and carbon air filter
- Dehumidifier
- Air fresheners (needed closer to harvest)
- Black/white tarp or Mylar
- Hooks and yarn, wire or fishing line (for dry room)
- Square pieces of lumber, to raise or lower plants under the lights
- Bungee cords, one foot long (for easy stowing of tarp covers when working)

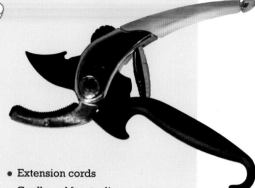

- Extension cords
- Cardboard for stapling up tarps
- Staple gun
- Vinegar/bleach for cleaning, plus scrub brush and scouring pads
  - Small scale to measure harvests
  - Tape measure to track growth
  - Grow journal (hard copy or computer, whichever is more secure and convenient for your purposes)
- Thermometer for temperature/humidity. Some can record daily highs/lows which is very useful

- Power bars (safety concerns)
- Timers that can work simultaneously in different rooms
- Green light (for when you need to go in there during dark periods)
- Big cutter (for harvest) and "nimble" scissors (for everything else)
- Rooting gel
- Rubbing alcohol (for sterilization) and paper towel for cleaning your garden scissors
- Rags for clean up
- Green bin (for daily culling of dead leaves, etc.)
- Gloves for plant maintenance and harvest to prevent contact highs
- Tape and Sharpie for labeling
- Lock for security
- Tubing for passive air flow
- Mason jars for curing/storage

Seeds ready for germination. Be sure to store unused seeds in a cool, dry, and dark place. An old coffee can with an airtight plastic lid is a great, nondescript container that won't warrant a second look.

Buy the Seed and Your Garden Will Grow

You may or may not be able to buy actual cannabis seeds at your local hydroponics outfit. Some stores stock all equipment needed to grow marijuana except for the actual marijuana itself. In many cities, it is possible to purchase seeds from a dedicated store. Depending on your personal connections, you might also be able to score seeds from a friend or compassion club if one is located nearby. These can be easily searched online or even through the many smartphone applications available for this and other purposes related to the cultivation and enjoyment of cannabis. You may also be able to buy seeds online. You will definitely want to grow from seed and avoid clones or even more mature plants unless you are dead positive that they are pest-free, and this is a difficult determination to make since few gardeners are going to invite you in for a peek, even if they are gracious enough to share some DNA.

It should go without saying, but you will want to buy a strain that is appropriate to both your grow situation and tastes. Some strains grow taller or wider than others. Some, like the appropriately named Skunk or Skunk crosses, are stinky, others almost without odor. Some are hardy and thus make good choice for beginners. Others are more fragile and even demanding in the requirements of their care. Then there is the matter of taste and effect. Even if you've been casually (or more seriously) enjoying marijuana for years, you may be unaware of the wide

This delicious Blueberry bud from OtherSide Farms showcases the strain's gorgeous structure and ample trichome production.

variety of "finishes" and effects available across strains. Appreciation of marijuana is not unlike sommeliers' classifications of fine wine. Some provide a "head" high, an effect amusingly described as "a good daytime pot, for the workday" by someone at a seed store I frequent. Others provide a definite "body" stone – something that can induce "couch lock" (yes, just like it sounds) if enjoyed in even a moderate dosage. Some strains are better for pain relief or stress reduction, others for sleep, still others for the stimulation of appetite. You might be looking for a specific combination of these effects depending on whether your purposes are medical, recreational or some combination of the two.

One thing is for certain: before you buy any seeds, do your research. Many seed sites online detail all of the above characteristics and some even give percentages of THC content, the ingredient that causes the much desired high. As with alcohol content, higher THC loads mean either a more serious high and/or the necessity to consume less to gain the desired effect. It's useful to consider the difference in kick between a beer (low content) to wine (mid content) to whisky (high content). THC levels in pot work on essentially the same principle. One truly excellent phone application is Leafly, or its online version, leafly.com. Both provide a strain guide with literally hundreds of different varieties, pictures, user reviews, assessments and described effects. It is a great place to start your search. This is a fun activity in itself, much like creating a wish list for Santa.

One other piece of advice I would offer when choosing a strain is that seeds will vary in price based upon several factors. These are availability, popularity and whether or not the seeds are "feminized." The first two are out of your control, but you will pay more for rare seeds and definitely for seeds that are the "it" strain at any given time. If you want to find strains that offer great value at reduced price, do an online search for "Cannabis Cup winners." The Cannabis Cup is an award given annually to the top strain or strains based on an internationally held competition within the marijuana cultivation community. Recent winners, like the Tangerine Dream that I will detail in this grow journal, will tend to be pricier. You can get good value however by searching for winners of previous years. Though their popularity will often have receded over time, they were good enough to be one-time winners. It doesn't matter that they are old news with the pros: they'll be new to you in any case. For instance, I really enjoy the Blueberry strain, but it is much cheaper than the newer Tangerine as it has been on the market for some time. Nonetheless, it is a fantastic smoke, grows beautifully and provides excellent value for money.

Feminization is a treatment that increases the chance that germinated seeds will produce female rather than male plants. Since females are the only gender that you will want to grow for now, feminized seeds are a plus. Males are necessary for strain development through generational genetic manipulation achieved by crossbreeding, but their presence at sexual maturity must be avoided when bringing cannabis plants to harvest. You will want to nuture the plump buds of unfertilized females without any male interference – and feminized seeds work! Though some will invariably produce male plants, as you will see from the grow I will profile, I had a 100% rate of female cultivation from seven seeds in three different (feminized) strains. This is much higher than the more typical 50-60% rate of female production that I have had in the past when growing from non-feminized seed, for instance, as in my trusted Master Kush. Whatever you purchase, be sure to buy at least four or five seeds of each strain so that you will definitely be able to produce multiple females.

One final consideration with respect to buying seeds and supplies: you may choose to pay in cash to reduce your "electronic footprint."

Be sure to account for daylight savings time. Check timers occasionally to ensure that everything is actually running according to schedule.

Bank statements and credit card bills may expose suspicious purchases, whereas cash leaves no trail, with no details about you. This may seem paranoid, but consider your own comfort level. If this is something that might keep you awake at night down the road, pay in cash. Growing marijuana should be relaxing and rewarding, not a source of stress.

If you follow the instructions in this book, you should be able to set up your room(s), buy all tools, supplies and seeds and start growing for under $1000, give or take. This initial investment can easily be recouped in the space of only a handful of grows. You will be saving money in no time, and having fun to boot.

Final Preparations

After storing your supplies, you will need to install your lights and set up timers. Be sure to test all electronic devices so that they are working smoothly before you crack open a single seed packet. Test lights before hanging by plugging into an outlet. Ensure that light ballasts (the metal appliance the light bulbs or tubes sit in) and reflectors have been wiped

The devil's in the details: take the time to set up your grow room well and you will avoid headaches later.

clean of fingerprints and dust. Lights should be hung from cables or light chains suspended from hooks that are secured well in a ceiling stud. This allows for easy movement of the lights: upwards as the plants grow toward them and downwards when they are removed and replaced with the next, much smaller generation to be brought to harvest. Check and recheck to ensure that lights are firmly secured – a fallen light is a costly mistake in its own right. It would also mean certain death for any plants underneath.

Timers should be set and checked to ensure that they are working accurately. If you have dedicated veg and bud rooms, you will need dedicated timers for the lights in each room. If you live in a jurisdiction that has different charges for electricity depending on the time of day, you might want to set timers to light the rooms during the cheapest periods possible, generally at night. You can avoid snagging wires by securing them well before you begin your grow, particularly if they will hang down (for instance if you must run an extension cord across a ceiling). Spend as much time as possible perfecting your setup, anticipating even the

Three cheers for green lights! A green spectrum LED flashlight is also a great tool to have on hand.

smallest problem, and this will go a long way to reducing headlines down the road. It will also increase your chances of enjoying a successful grow.

There is one other light, a non-specialized one, in which you will want to invest. A green spectrum light for the area just outside your grow room(s) is a must if at all possible. Cheap and widely available, a green bulb is necessary for those times that you must access your garden when one or both parts are in their dark cycle. This is something that all gardeners must do from time to time, for instance, if you need to water plants early when leaving for an overnight trip. Having this light and a couple of spare bulbs on hand is a great decision to make. When your green bulb burns out after the stores are closed and you desperately need to get into your grow room while it's dark, you'll be thankful that you thought ahead.

Small fans should be present in each grow room. If you have vented your room(s) (in a light-tight way, see diagram: venting your grow room) to allow for passive air exchange as you should have, fans aren't necessary, strictly speaking. However, they provide important air circulation

Lighting Considerations

The first question for the new grower is what type of lights to purchase. Whatever type you ultimately select, ensure that they are equipped with a reflective hood to maximize light absorption. White polyethylene sheeting to increase the overall reflectivity of the room is also a must.

There are four main considerations in choosing lighting apparatus:

1. Wattage or "lumens" of light produced. Generally, more is better and will increase your yield. However, more is not always better.

2. Cost of the light. You will want to purchase the best, most efficient light you can afford. The best light is likely the one that will best maximize the size of your grow room or closet. Important: never, never, never skimp on lights that may be unsafe. A burned down home is your worst grow result of all time!

3. The amount of energy required to operate your light. Remember that these lights will be on most of the time. You should calculate how much new lights will add to your energy bill on a monthly basis. Also, keep in mind that as a security consideration, increased energy use is more likely to raise suspicion from authorities. For this reason, growing with T5 fluorescent lights is more secure than HPS and other more powerful lighting systems - they are less likely to cause telltale energy spikes on 18/12 and 12/12 cycles that a utility company might be tracking.

4. Heat produced by the light. A high amount of heat energy released is inefficient in terms of energy use; though it can warm a cool grow room. However, too much heat may require you to use additional fans or air conditioners to reduce room temperatures. This can be a hassle, is costly, and may not be an option depending on your grow conditions. As a rule, I would suggest that it is easier to warm your rooms than to cool them.

Obviously, increased wattage/lumens produced increases your grow potential. However, the hotter the light, the further plants must be moved away from it, which of course reduces the amount of lumens received. This might seem like a Catch-22, so what is the solution?

I would suggest a good T5 light. Although a T5 is a fluorescent light, it is the highest efficiency fluorescent.

This is decidedly not your typical industrial fluorescent. The advantages of the T5 make it an easy choice: it produces more than sufficient lumens to conduct a successful grow with impressive yields. It is both cheaper to purchase and (much) cheaper to operate than High Intensity Discharge (HID), High Pressure Sodium (HPS) or Metal Halide (MH) lamps. These ones are for the "pros" and are overkill for most home grows. Given how much heat these lights produce, they also present the potential of an increased fire risk when compared to T5s, a real consideration if you are growing in cramped conditions. Also, because the T5s are so much cooler (and don't require a separate ballast system that adds to setup cost, energy use and heat generated), you can snuggle your plants very close underneath them. This maximizes light exposure and absorption, and makes up for being less powerful compared to their more traditionally used cousins.

What's the downside? Keeping your plants close to the lights can cause burns if you don't check your plants frequently. Checking them is a daily job and can be a bit of extra work jockeying lights around on chains and/or moving shelves around to most effectively situate the plants. Still, this is the safest, cheapest, easiest setup for most novices. Even the sales staff at my local hydroponics store advised I go this route when I got started, and they were giving up the possibility of me purchasing a more expensive light setup. I continue to appreciate their honesty and good advice!

You will also want to purchase both "warm" and "cool" bulbs. The former are in the red light spectrum and are meant for use in the bud room, the latter are in the blue spectrum, and are meant for vegetative growth. Though these will last for months at a time, it is a good idea to have several spares of each on hand, in case you lose a light to burn out when your local hydroponics store is closed or otherwise inaccessible.

With lights assembled and installed in the grow room(s), they must be put on timers. Marijuana will grow or "vegetate" without budding when in light for more than twelve hours per day. The exception to this are "auto-flowering" strains, which come with other pros and cons. We will consider these more fully elsewhere.

When the plants are reduced to a cycle of twelve hours of light, twelve hours of darkness, they will begin the process through full maturity to budding. Why? Because this light schedule approximates the end of a natural outdoor growing season, when the plants usually bud. This is where you'll finally be able to see the bud you're doing all this work to produce.

That's it. You're lit up and ready to grow.

This passive air vent is light-tight. It is curved behind the polyethylene tarp to ensure light gets neither in nor out, but allows for the intake of air to replace that which is vented outside.

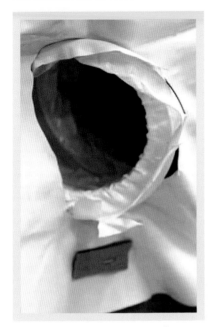

Note the tube curving away from the hole. A snake behind the curtain is your goal here.

Plastic shelves with adjustable leg heights are an easy way to maintain short and taller plants under a single light source.

and promote growth of strong stems by forcing plants to strain against the air currents they create. Moreover, they will moderate temperatures if things get too hot in your grow rooms. They're cheap, they're quiet and they are easy. Use them.

The final task is also one of the most potentially labor intensive: venting the grow room. The best way to ensure even, regular circulation of new air into your rooms is to install a venting fan. These fans can (and should) be attached to drums that contain carbon filters. When used in conjunction with one another, these two things will reduce the telltale odors associated with marijuana to nearly zero. Ideally, you will be able to vent your room to the outside. Most units are fairly quiet; mine can be heard only faintly in the next room and outside is inaudible from about five feet away. Close up, it sounds similar to the vent from a furnace or dryer. In fact, if you can place it in close proximity to one of these, this is a great cover. Carbon filters generally need

Room Setup

1. Check the maximum height that you'll have for growth. At least four feet clearance is ideal. Remember that lights will hang down from the ceiling, reducing the amount of room plants have to grow vertically.

2. Locate studs and install hooks from which lights will be hung. Attach chains on which to hang/ move lights. Check that chains will hang easily on hooks BEFORE you buy (i.e. that chain loops are wide enough to fit over the hooks).

3. In the case of concrete floors, cover with plywood or some other insulating material that can be cleaned easily when spills occur.

4. Install ventilation from the exterior grate into the grow room for passive air flow. Snake the ventilation tubing so that no light escapes from either end of the grate.

5. Staple polyethylene tightly onto the walls. Use cardboard pieces to avoid ripping.

6. Hang a thermometer so that temperatures can be monitored easily and a green light bulb for working during times when the lights must be kept off.

If possible, buy a thermometer that measures relative humidity as well as temperature. Some units will record daily highs/lows: this is invaluable for seeing how hot/cold your rooms are running at times you aren't there.

7. Place fans in appropriate locations, out of the way.

8. Install exhaust fan and carbon filter in Bud Room. Follow manufacturer's instructions. If possible, vent to the outdoors.

9. Secure all wires. Minimize risk of wires falling into water. Power bars and timers should sit well clear of your grow area.

10. Install a lock and/or camouflage your grow room. Trust no one!

11. Create a work area outside the grow room if possible. It's a plus, as is a dedicated drying area.

12. Ensure that cleaning supplies are ready for use. Review how to "clean up" your area: can you sweep the area directly outside your grow rooms clean of all evidence of your hobby in five minutes or less? This should be your goal, in case of an emergency.

to be replaced every 12 to 24 months. They are invaluable for keeping your daily grow as a secret garden. The only other consideration is that your vent fan should be placed in the bud room if at all possible. Plants in the veg room will produce little if any smell since they are sexually immature. It is only the valuable bud that will stink. If you will be placing budding plants in a veg room (for instance, in the case of growing

Happy cannabis, with buds starting to plump up under the warm embrace of T5 fluorescents.

autoflowering strains which benefit from a more continuous light cycle, even when flowering), you should create a vent between rooms and ensure that a small fan moves air out of the veg room and into the bud room for expulsion.

The only other consideration in terms of room setup is ensuring that floors are warm, at least moderately so. Cold floors, such as concrete floors in a basement, can stunt plant growth. A thin layer of plywood or plastic shelves placed between plant trays and concrete is all that is required. Warming mats and the like are for the most part an unnecessary expense.

The room is built. The materials have been purchased. Setup is complete. Now, we're ready to start our grow. Onward!

Your Daily Grow

Before you start your grow, take a deep breath, and

remember this: moving slowly, deliberately, and with

patience will generally serve you well as you cultivate your

garden. Hopefully, you won't often face emergency

situations, but if you do, you will want to be as prepared as

possible – with supplies for example. Taking decisive, timely

action will be necessary of course. However, the best action

is often the one you don't take, or the mistake you don't

make. It is easier to respond slowly to solve problems as

they arise rather than undoing something you have done in

haste. With that advice in mind, I'm ready to start a new crop

in my grow rooms. I will be both cloning Master Kush from

my Kush Mother and germinating new plants from seed.

Seed Germination

1. Select and obtain seeds for strain(s) that are appropriate to the conditions of your grow room and "bud objectives" (effects when consumed).

2. Germination will take roughly 2-3 days from removing from packaging to being ready to plant in soil. Plan your time accordingly.

3. Best method: moisten (not soak) a paper towel, fold, and place on a plate. Use standard paper towel with no chemicals on it.

4. Place seeds into paper towel. Cover with fold over. Cover plate with Saran Wrap to hold in moisture.

5. Place covered plate somewhere dark and warm, like a desk drawer.

6. Minimize exposure of germinating seeds to light, particularly when they have sprung a root.

7. Check daily.

8. Once seeds have begun to sprout noticeably – a little tail is what you are looking for – transplant into soil. Don't wait too long or the seeds will die. Once they've sprung the shell they need access to the moisture and nutrients that soil provide.

9. Transplant into slightly moistened soil by placing one finger into the soil to the first knuckle then placing the seed into the hole. Be careful not to plant too deep.

10. The "tail" MUST POINT DOWN!

11. Place seedling pods as close to lights as possible so that seedlings will not stretch when they emerge.

12. Check daily until seedlings pop clear of the soil. Water as necessary – soil should be moist but not water-logged. Soil will dry out quickly when in close proximity to lights.

13. When watering seedlings use only demineralized water, not tap until they are fully formed seedlings, for the first week or two. This minimizes the chance that water used will have an unsuitable pH and stress the fragile seedlings.

14. Seedlings require no nutrients until much later in the growing process. Nutrients should be added to their feed slowly and at very low concentrations at first.

15. Resist the urge to remove seed casings that have not fallen off seedlings. They will fall off on their own as they grow. Taking them off by hand can rip fragile seedlings.

16. It is crucial to label seeds at the time of planting. A bit of masking tape and a Sharpie are all that is required. Record the date planted and the strain, particularly if planting several strains simultaneously and in close proximity. Apply tape to appropriate seed pod. Transfer labels to successively larger pots with each transplant.

17. If one or more seeds don't germinate, try again with new seeds to hit your desired number. Keep in mind that you will likely have to kill some (males) as even feminized seeds provide no absolute guarantee of female plants.

Day 1

You may be tempted to skip the step of germinating from seed, possibly due to the fact that the cost can run into the hundreds of dollars depending on the strain you are growing. You might be tempted to obtain a clone if one or more is available. However, germination is quick, dead easy and has one inarguable advantage over importing a clone from another garden: with seed, it is impossible to import problems (such as pests) into your own garden – and this can often happen when importing clones from elsewhere. Unless you are positive about the grow conditions of a sourced clone, don't go there – cleaning up the mess of a problem-laden clone is far more trouble than the few minutes it will take you over a few days to germinate the seeds.

Label plants to avoid mix ups. It is useful to include cloning/ germination and expected harvest dates, as well as strain. For cloned plants, you may also wish to indicate sex so that you know which plants must be watched more or less closely during early weeks of budding.

The new strain I've selected to grow is Tangerine Dream. I have purchased five feminized seeds and will start by germinating three. I have also been given a single seed from a third strain, Pandora, as a gift. I've decided to give it a whirl too, though it will be a one shot deal. I won't be saving it for future cultivation (and couldn't in any case because it is an autoflowering seed – more on that later).

After putting the seeds away in a warm dark drawer, on a plate covered in damp paper towel and Saran Wrap, I am ready to move on to cloning.

This is far more labor intensive. As it is a process best done in several distinct steps, I make sure to set up and check over all necessary materials prior to going anywhere near Mother Kush with scissors: demineralized water in a spray bottle, measuring cup, rooting gel, soil and pods for planting and of course the scissors. Whether you use scissors or a

Germination 101: starting from seed is a snap with the right gear.

razor, be sure to sterilize them before cutting. This is important so that you don't unwittingly transfer a problem from one plant to another. You may not even know that a problem exists – but it is unwise to take chances with your garden, however small, after you've invested much time and energy. Thus, I have cleaned these scissors, which were covered in sticky resin from the just-completed harvest. Rubbing alcohol and a paper towel do the job nicely.

Though I mostly garden alone, I've invited my partner Ms. Woodward to join me and help with the cloning. We look over the Kush Mother and pick three healthy stems, each approximately four to five inches in length with healthy growth and leaf development. We only cut one at a time, however; not all three at once. It is important to complete each clone as quickly as possible because having one or two cuttings sitting and waiting while exposed to the air while you finish transplanting your first clone isn't a good idea.

The cut is made below new growth to give the new plant a maximized chance at successfully taking off. About four to eight inches long is best, as cuttings any shorter will not have sufficient size to grow, or

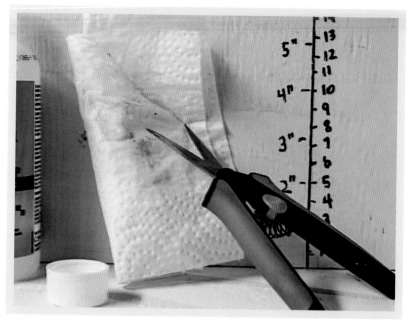

Clean scissors after every use, particularly when cloning new plants. A high strength rubbing alcohol is better than the standard drug store brand for removing sticky resin.

at least will take much longer to mature. The longer a cutting/clone is, the more difficulty the plant will have maintaining itself without roots, while the root structure develops. This will take two weeks or more, so making a cutting of medium size is better than being over-ambitious. Remember to leave approximately one inch to be submerged in soil. Even a light cutting requires a firm base.

Ultimately, like most aspects of a daily grow, cloning is a matter of trial and (learning from) error. There isn't a hard and fast rule about the "right" way to do anything. Instead, it is better to proceed using anything you read or are told about growing marijuana, including the advice in this guide, as a place to start. Every grow situation is unique and thus so is every grow. While there are some "basics" that a new grower such as yourself will likely have good success with, growing cannabis is, in my opinion, equal parts art and science.

When starting something new, gather information from different sources – but don't expect one correct answer. Many debates continue

New clones are placed in water. It is good practice to remove a glob of gel from the container rather than dipping stems directly into the gel container. Doing the latter 'activates' the unused gel, making it less effective for future cloning.

Cuttings are submerged in water on the cut end, then cut again, on a diagonal, while under water. The clone-to-be is then ready for rooting gel.

to rage about the best or at least different ways to approach many different aspects of a daily grow, from ways to clone to maximizing yield. Grow books such as this one are a good place to start (much of my initial reading on the subject came from *The Cannabis Grow Bible*, Greg Green's indispensible handbook for serious gardeners, also available from Green Candy Press). Because this book is written for newbies, from the perspective of a new-ish gardener, it should answer most questions you will face as you move through your first grow from seed to harvest. But the many grow sites on the Internet, particularly the many pot discussion boards, are excellent resources for getting new ideas, second opinions or for that problem situation that you aren't sure how to handle. If you're facing a tricky situation, other passionate gardeners will have too, and may have posted their experiences online.

Back to cloning: after I've made the cut, the cutting is placed directly into a water-filled glass measuring cup. It can rest here while the next steps are taken. The rooting gel is opened and prepared. The soil, our growth medium of choice for all things, is ladled into the seedling pods and pre-moistened. I am sure to use the demineralized water that has been made ready for this purpose. I make a small indented hole in the soil with my index finger to prepare the soil. We are now ready for the final, most crucial stage: second cut and transplant.

Although the initial cut was straight across the stem (the angle for the first cut doesn't matter, only the second is crucial), the next cut must be made at a forty-five degree angle. This is a must! When I first started cloning, I lost half a dozen cuttings because I skipped this step. Everything else had been done correctly, and the clones would live for a week, even two. But then they consistently wilted, browned and died over a couple of days. The reason: no root formations grew, even after adjusting for temperature, light exposure and trying multiple grow mediums (soil, rock wool, a cup filled with damp paper towel). The angled cut acts as a catalyst to promote generation of new roots. Take care with this step.

Don't worry too much about this: once you are aware of the correct cutting method, this isn't difficult. Some people will suggest a razor blade for the second cut rather than scissors. However, if you purchase a set of high-quality fine scissors, this isn't really necessary. In fact, I find

Save a used gel jar to use for making clones without activating a full jar.

Fresh clones can look a little mangled, but don't despair: it's called 'weed' for a reason.

working with a naked razor to be more finicky, and it requires placing the cutting flat on a cutting board to get enough purchase for a clean cut. Even with a clean board, this opens your new plant to a greater chance of contamination. Why bother? A free hand cut with scissors is quick and easy – and it can be done under water to minimize the chance of an air bubble entering the exposed stem.

From here, I remove the clone from the water and dip into rooting gel, ensuring that I have covered the cutting tip generously. I try to get as much on as I can without it dripping off. With this done, the clone is placed in the soil indent and I cover it with soil, firming the soil base up around the stem. Take care with this step to ensure that you don't inadvertently wipe off the rooting gel by scraping it into an unopened patch of soil. It is much better to move the soil around the cutting rather than moving the cutting through packed soil.

We're almost done now. The final step is to trim lower fan leaves to leave sufficient space between the lower leaves and the soil. Leaves that drag in the soil will die. Moreover, even fewer than half a dozen

New clones are placed carefully in the growing medium: soil. A paper towel underneath reduces clean up from water, but cloning can be done in a pan as well.

fan leaves placed higher on the cutting will more than serve your purposes. This can also be done before cutting and gelling the new clone; whatever works for you! I put this new Kush clone aside and continue with my next two, repeating the process each time.

When all three are planted, inspected and ready to go, they are placed in a pan and spritzed with demineralized water. Demineralized water has two advantages: it is cheap (less than two bucks at my local grocery for a four gallon container) and it has a neutral pH, which is essential if, like most new growers, you are unsure about the pH of your tap water. Testing pH can be an expensive undertaking; pro kits range into the hundreds of dollars. Better are pH testing strips which can be purchased at most garden centers. These will be the same the kind you probably used back in a junior high science class when learning about acid versus base solutions. Cannabis is best cultivated in soil using water with a pH rating of 6-7 (7 is neutral, lower than 7 is more acidic, higher is more base or alkaline). Hydroponic setups require slightly lower pH water, but as a new grower you'll likely want to steer away from the

Note the relatively short height of these clones. They are all set and ready for their new home.

higher cost and technical training needed to set up a hydroponic oper-ation. For my garden I have always used demineralized water for seeds and clones for the first couple weeks, until such time as the new plants are looking healthy enough, then I switch to tap water (which the testing strips show as being somewhere between pH 6 and 7, just fine for the novice grower). Monkeying with pH can be expensive and time consum-ing; why bother if you don't need to? You will probably only want to go there if you hit a serious problem with growth that could be pH-based.

New clones are fragile. Until root structures form, the plants are only able to get water through their leaves. Therefore, I spritz the plants lib-erally, and even daily for the first several days in warm conditions (during the summer, for instance). Even in cooler conditions, as soon as they ap-pear dry, I spritz them again, giving each plant a good soak. After three to five days, I start weaning the clones off scheduled spritzing, in time with developing roots assuming responsibility for hydrating the plants.

I place a plastic bubble over the pan to keep the new plants warm and to reduce evaporation. They are put into their new home, inside

A little water in the pan before placing under the bubble never hurts – it helps maintain high humidity beneficial to fragile clones.

Clones should be further away from lights compared to more mature plants. Stretching isn't a worry until new growth is well under way.

A few days later, new clones are standing tall. Spritzing is now reduced to promote root growth. If you keep spritzing, root development can be delayed.

the veg room, on a plastic shelf off the floor; it is important to ensure that these most vulnerable plants are warm, so direct contact with a concrete floor should be avoided. They will sit approximately two feet below the T5 fluorescent lights. If everything goes well, these three are about two weeks from viability, measured by the presence of roots, and will be transplanted for two to five weeks more vegetative growth before moving to a reduced light cycle for flowering. All vegging plants require enough time to grow calyx formations on stems in order to provide locations for eventual bud development (which is of course the whole point and thus our goal). Beyond this basic requirement, however, the time for maturation in the vegetative state largely depends on two factors: The first is how big you want plants

Guide to Cloning

1. Ideal candidate stems will be four to eight inches in length. Optimum length is six inches but experiment with this.

2. Stems should be healthy and strong but not "woody." Stems that are too thick and have a hardened epidermis are unsuitable for cloning.

3. Lower branches are best but any healthy branch stem will do in a pinch.

4. Trim fan leaves from the lower two or three inches of the stem to be cloned. This can be done before or after the clone is cut.

5. When starting out, grow clones in soil. Rockwool grow mediums or aeroponic cloning systems can be excellent, but neither is ideal or in fact necessary for the novice grower (the former is more appropriate for hydroponic grows, the latter is an advanced cloning technique). Start in soil since clones will be staying in soil.

6. Demineralized water is essential through cloning process until root structure is established. Once roots are established it is okay to switch to tap water.

7. Spritz leaves daily for the first two to four days so that the leaves don't wither and die. At this time, experiment with reducing spritzing. Once stems and leaves remain firm with reduced or no spritzing, it can be stopped altogether.

8. Warm, humid grow conditions are best. Clones should not be cultivated too close to lights as they will dry out too quickly – they lack roots necessary to hydrate plants close to the heat of lights.

9. Initially, use a bubble to hold moisture/humidity. This can be ended after a week or less.

10. Process: clean scissors with alcohol to sterilize – don't pass on any

to be before moving them into the bud stage. This is something you will need to experiment with based on the typical size of the strain/s you are growing and the limitations of your grow room. The second factor is the number of interventions in your plants' natural growing time you plan to make in order to maximize yields. Techniques such as topping and super cropping (that will be discussed later) will slow down and extend the vegetative growth period. However, my experience is that the patience required to make a few interventions to maximize bud production is time and effort well spent. It is also a fun aspect to play and experiment with: don't be surprised if you quickly become passionate about methods to propagate bigger and better plants – and harvests!

problems to new plants.

11. Some guides suggest use of a razor for the second diagonal cut (at 45 degrees) that follows the straight cut from the Mother Plant. A razor is not strictly necessary for second cut. Just cut on angle using fine scissors. This cut can also be accomplished under water (see below).

12. Use a measuring cup filled with demineralized water to eliminate the danger of air bubbles entering the cut stem. Place the cutting into the water after removing from the Mother.

13. Optional: gently scrape the lowest half-inch of the cutting to eliminate the outer epidermis. This will promote root development.

14. Rooting gel is a must. Avoid powder. Coat the cutting's end generously in gel.

15. Do one clone at a time to avoid mistakes and minimize the time it takes. Minimize stress wherever you can!

16. Trim excess leaves. Use rooting gel. Push a finger into soil and place the seed into the hole. Cover with soil and make sure it is solid.

17. Repeat with all clones.

18. Spritz and place into bubble.

19. Watch and spritz daily.

20. Mistakes to avoid: straight cut. Not placing directly into water. Inappropriate cutting choice. Not having everything laid out and ready to go BEFORE you start cutting.

21. Remember to label your clones. Even once you are experienced enough to distinguish between strains by eye, you should still label plants – and different phenotypes of the same plant, so you can select the strongest clones to propagate. Dates provide important information down the road. Be sure to indicate the (female) gender of sexed clones, as distinguished from unsexed plants germinated from seeds.

These Master Kush plants have outgrown their pots. Unless you are aiming for a Bonsai-style plant, which can be okay for a quicker if less bountiful harvest, roots need room to spread out.

Day 2

After all the activity yesterday, I can take it easier today. It is important to keep this in mind: to avoid problems before they develop, it is advantageous to plan your gardening a few days ahead of schedule whenever possible. Much like an expert chess player wins because she is planning several moves ahead, a successful gardener is well served by planning. It allows you to purchase and prepare materials in advance of course, and leads to fewer errors caused by hasty action. Also, it gives you a chance to plan your activities to balance your time; remember that life outside the garden can intrude to the detriment of your plants. If you have organized your grow activities to account for days when you will have more or less time, or more or less labor-intensive tasks planned, you will likely be more successful (and happier).

With that in mind, yesterday I chose to defer transplanting the two Master Kush clones into their final home: three-gallon pots. These were actually overdue for a transplant, a fact confirmed by the dense,

The bigger pot is filled with soil and moistened. See how much more room the plants will have now.

Tap the plant out of its pot. It's cannabis, not a carrot! Massage the root ball to prepare it and tamp down firmly in new soil so that it has a solid base from which to grow.

The Master Kushes in their new, roomier homes. They could use another week or two in vegetative growth, but with new plants on the way, they've been moved to flowering.

crowded root structures of each plant when I take them out of their one-gallon pots today.

I prepare each pot in advance, lining the bottom of each with paper. This keeps the soil from falling out of the holes in the pots, but allows excess water to run out into the pans. This is an absolute must! When growing in soil, don't use old flowerpots that lack drainage holes. Plastic pots of various sizes and shapes, with holes, are cheap and readily available at garden centers and hydro stores. They can also be reused with washing and sterilization so they are a good eco option.

Once lined, I fill each of the larger pots with soil, moistening it as per the soil's instructions, and dig out appropriate sized holes to place each plants' root structure into.

I tap the bottom of each pot smartly to loosen the roots. When each releases, I gently slide the plant out of the pot. The bottom of each plant has the paper, which lined the one-gallon pots they've outgrown, still attached to the roots. I carefully pick as much of this out as possible, without causing serious damage to the roots themselves.

Clones should be sprayed liberally and daily for the first few days after cutting.

These Kush clones enjoy a little light but not too much.

Note the humidity on the inside of the bubble. This is what you want to see: optimum conditions for successful cloning.

Following this, I place the plant into the soil and cover, firming up the soil base. I do this while attempting to minimize exposure of the roots to light.

Since these two Kush haven't been fed in almost a week, I give them a feed today, splitting two liters between the two plants. I follow the Transition nutrient schedule a second time (the first was done in the veg room, in anticipation of this move). I will stay on this nutrient mixture until the buds begin to form. Note that this isn't ideal: transplanting from pot to pot itself stresses plants. Moreover, the move to the bud room is a big change since the plants will no doubt be shocked somewhat by the sudden change from an 18/6 to 12/12 light schedule – stress number two. I've now added a third stress by feeding directly after transplanting. That said, the plants are healthy and shouldn't suffer too much from this. The main danger here is not that the plants will die, but that they could respond to major stress by changing from female (as I've cloned these Kush from a sexed "Mother" plant, I am 100% certain that the clones will also be female, 100% of the time, when they display sex) to hermaphrodites – plants that would then have to be trashed, to make sure that the male part of the hermies don't infect my bud room with pollen, ruining the crop.

The cuttings taken yesterday look unchanged. I give them a minor spritz and leave them alone. Similarly, the seeds have not sprung any roots yet, which is unsurprising after only a day. I lightly moisten the paper towel they are in with dribbles of water applied gently and non-directly on the seeds themselves.

Covered, they are returned to their dark drawers until tomorrow. Note that I have labeled them by strain to avoid confusion down the road. A little goof here could lead to major issues down the road – there's no sense in mixing the babies up at the hospital!

Day 3

There are no changes to be made to the two Kush today. That said, this is a good opportunity to take some notes with initial observations. Why? A running, even very brief daily grow journal is essential for two reasons. First, it will allow you to improve from grow to grow; you will

Here, lights have been raised at one end to accommodate the taller of the two plants. This sort of adjustment is a daily or semi-daily job during vegetation and the first few weeks of flowering.

want to be able to review what worked, in order to replicate it in later grows, and the results of experiments and happy mistakes can shape your cultivation practice. Secondly, having a base standard is important for the sake of comparison. This is a must when you run into problems, and ultimately even the luckiest gardener will have some problems. When this happens, you might be surprised that you won't necessarily be able to recall the state of individual plants, even a few days prior to the day on which you encounter a potential problem. Writing down information before running into difficulties can be invaluable in helping to solve them. This will be less and less necessary over time but is definitely a good idea for your first few grows. In fact, a grow journal can make the difference when you have to determine whether a problem exists, find out to what extent it exists and solve it.

I record some basic measurements and qualities of the plants today and leave it at that. Aside from anecdotal daily notes of a very brief nature, I tend to do a weekly update to chart changes in development. For the more technologically advanced, several grow journal applications

This Kush has numerous calyxes that are crucial for bud formation. Keeping plants snugged up to the light while vegging is the key: instead of stretched plants, multiple bud sites form.

Though still too early for new growth, these clones are responding well and look to be on track.

are available for most smart phones and tablets. However, you should ask yourself this before using such tools: how secure is your device? If kids or colleagues might inadvertently stumble on your grow journal while borrowing your phone, is that a conversation you are prepared to have? You might find a simple old school pen and pad of paper stored with your grow tools and nutrients is more secure and just as effective for staying on top of what is happening in your garden.

Over in the veg room, I give the clones a good soak. Note the humidity present in the bubble. I check the seeds sitting in their drawer: no action yet but I will likely see this in the next day or two.

Day 4

Today is a big day: three of the four seeds have "popped" and clearly show a white root tendril protruding from the seed shell. I could probably wait until tomorrow to plant these, but it is best to get these in

Press one knuckle deep into moistened soil.

Hold the seed casing lightly as you place the tail down into the hole you've made.

the soil as soon as possible. There's no sense in waiting for the fourth seed, which, I suspect, may be dead. I'll give it another couple of days and then start a new seed germinating if it doesn't pop. I don't do this straight away because I don't want to waste a seed, and will if I start a replacement seed and this one pops a bit late (I'm limited by the size constraints of my grow rooms, so I am mindful not to unnecessarily burn seeds which are expensive. This is not a problem once you are at the cloning stage, as these are easily replaced and can be weeded out selectively to allow for propagation of the strongest specimens). I will wait a little longer before pulling the plug on the un-hatched seed.

I take the seeds out of the drawer but leave them wrapped up and in low light exposure until the seedpods are prepared with moist soil and small holes for implantation. Afterward, I plant them, being careful to place them in the soil with the roots pointed down, into the soil. This is easy enough for even an experienced grower to forget (I myself had to consult my notes as I've been cloning for some time and this is my first seed ger-

Newly planted seeds should be placed close to lights to avoid stretching. However, unless you can check on them daily until moved into proper pots, further away may be necessary to avoid scorching them. Trial and error is your best guide here.

mination in months). It might seem logical for the seed to be placed in with the tendril turned up to grow out of the soil. This is backwards, however, and would jeopardize the viability of these very valuable (and expensive) seeds. Remember: roots should point DOWN to the ground.

After covering them, I place these in a pan in the veg room. However, unlike the clones, which require a two-foot gap from the lights while at the sensitive root-generation stage, the germinated seeds can, and should, be put as close to the lights as possible. Failure to do so can lead to ugly (and dangerous) stretching. The plants from my very first grow looked like mutants all the way through their life cycle because they spent a few days at this initial development stage too far from the lights and stretched to meet them, resulting in very long stems with a reduced number of calyxes and bud formations. Keep your seedlings as close as possible to the lights, leaving a few inches so that the plants can emerge from the soil without danger of hitting the lights themselves.

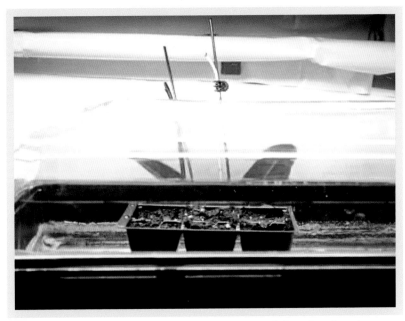

Striking a balance: these seedlings-to-be will spend their first few days under the bubble but as close as possible to the lights.

Note that I have labeled one pod with a "P" on tape to differentiate the Pandora seed from the two Tangerine seeds.

Otherwise, this was a pretty slow day and I had some extra time on my hands so I decide to give both grow rooms a good clean with vinegar and sweep/vacuum up. This too is a good practice to get in the habit of – it reduces the chance of pest infestations. It also makes your garden more pleasant to work in and less conspicuous to visitors who might observe vegetative debris that's tough to explain.

Day 5

Today there is evidence of stress on the fan leaves of the Kush that were transplanted and moved yesterday. They are slightly yellowed, with a red, rash-like look developing. In retrospect, I shouldn't have fed the plants at the same time as transplanting and moving to the 12/12 light cycle. It would have been better to simply water when making the

Keep an eye on the vigor of fan leaves. They are your early warning
signals of stress or nutrient deficiencies. Note the spotting here.

Accurate labels are critical for navigating your garden intelligently.

Keep soil pods moist but not soaked by watering frequently in small amounts.

move, then feed even a day or two later. I will have to monitor their health closely for the next few days.

To minimize the effects of the feed, I split a quart of water between the two plants. Given that the soil is still moist, there is a fair amount of run-off into the pan. I've done the right thing, but backwards. This is something I won't repeat in the future.

Over in the veg room, the seeds have yet to pop out of the soil. It is very dry though, so I dribble on some demineralized water. These should emerge in the next couple of days.

The cuttings continue to look good. The leaves are deep green with no necrosis. I spritz them again and check to ensure that their soil remains slightly moist. There isn't much point in watering the soil beyond this, since the plants don't have the roots to make use of the soil. The goal at this point is simply to keep the conditions comfortable for the cuttings until the roots do develop.

To ensure this, I keep them in a bubble to trap the humidity. I also ensure that the cuttings are a couple of feet below the lights; too close

These fan leaves are healthy. Note where problems occur: nutrient deficiencies often appear first on lower leaves, while light burns occur higher up.

and they will burn easily since they lack roots necessary to hydrate the leaves after transpiration of moisture caused by proximity to warm lights. Even T5 fluorescents throw off a fair bit of heat close up. Further away is better at this point.

Day 6

Some positive signs in the bud room today: the first signs of growth. The smaller of the two plants is too close to the light. Rather than move the lights, a quicker solution is to move the plants to the left since that side is higher. This is a time saver – moving the plants around when you can is often quicker than monkeying with light chains. Moreover, it is good for the plants since it changes up the light distribution day-to-day, which promotes more even growth in all parts of the plant and avoids problems like leaning, which is caused by plants growing, un-moved, toward a stationary light source. Remember that the lights

Turn plants every day or two in a consistent direction e.g. Clockwise a quarter turn. This helps plants to grow evenly rather than growing lopsided toward the lights.

mimic the sun but don't move like it – you have to do this for the plants.

The Kush's soil is still quite wet – it clumps when I take a pinch in my hand and is almost the consistency of mud. Best to take a break from watering. Otherwise, they look good. The yellowing doesn't seem to have progressed, so hopefully they are getting over the stress of the last few days. I nip one fan leaf that looks too yellow to be saved. There's no point in having the plant pour resources into damaged bits that are too far gone to grow healthy.

Over in the veg room, the cuttings look fine. I soak the leaves again and replace the bubble, though I do open the vent holes slightly to release some moisture and moderate the humidity.

The exciting development for today is that the three seeds have broken the soil and are between an inch and one and a half inches high. This happened, quickly, over just one night. Each has a set of four 'fetal' leaves (cotyledon is biological term but that's a bit technical for me); they are oval, not shaped like cannabis leaves. Once the plants develop, these will yellow, brown and eventually fall off within a couple weeks.

And we're off to the races! Tangerine seedlings emerge from the soil.

Too moist to require more water for now. Don't be afraid to get your hands dirty.

Slight yellowing: keep your eyes peeled to observe potentially problematic developments.

For now, the development looks great.

One important note for a new grower: don't touch any seed shells that remain on the tops of new seedlings. One of the Tangerines has a casing stuck to the top, but I leave it be. They pose no danger to seedling development and will fall off naturally. Trying to remove them manually could result in an untimely rip to tender new leaves. Look, but don't touch!

Checking in with the seeds germinating in the drawer, the fourth Tangerine Dream seed has now popped, so I transplant it into soil with the first three. Provided it develops further, this will bring my seedling count to one Pandora and three Tangerines.

Allowing gradual airflow lets clones adjust to conditions they will face outside the bubble. Note that humidity has dissipated.

Wait until seeds have popped before placing in soil.

That's more like it!

This officially marks the end of the original seed that never developed. In a case like this, you may want to check with whomever you purchased your seeds from. Some sellers will stand by their seeds and give replacement seeds for those that don't develop. I called and checked with the store where I bought mine and they said that I could return this seed for a replacement, provided I save the packaging and receipt. I have saved both. One important note here regarding security: I have a secure (locked) box that I keep outside my grow room to store any grow-related materials like receipts and the dead seed. I don't want to lose track of any of this or, worse, have a visiting friend or family member stumble upon it inadvertently. That is one discussion I would rather not have.

My gardening is largely a private affair and yours should be too – resist the urge to brag about your new grow (I was advised against it and still I did it, to a handful of people I trust. In retrospect however, I wish I had kept my mouth shut). The fewer people who know what you are doing, the better. You might trust them, but who might they talk to casually? People you might not know, or trust. Discretion is key – you can never take back talking about your garden.

Day 7

The Master Kush plants in the bud room continue to look better and better. Their color is looking more green and healthy. Though their soil remains moist, I push an extra half-quart of water into each pot to finalize the flush. This may be overdoing it but I'd rather err on the side of caution, and being slightly overwatered will hurt the plants less than stress caused by a poorly timed feed on Day Two.

Over in the veg room, I water the Kush Mother and cull a small handful of yellowed leaves from throughout the plant. It is over six months old,

The race is on. Pandora and Tangerine Dream seedlings are indistinguishable in the early days.

and bushy, so leaves dying from time to time is normal. Pruning the mother to ensure that it doesn't grow into the lights, and doesn't get so thick at the top that light doesn't penetrate into the bottom of the plant, is normal, weekly maintenance.

Considering the three seedlings today, I'm a little concerned that they might be stretching. To address this, I remove the small bubble and add several boards under their pan to move them as close to the lights as possible. The pan is now almost snug up against the sides. This will require a close eye for the next few days: if I don't check often, the fragile seedlings could have a growth spurt and hit the lights. While this would not be the end of the world even a couple weeks into a grow, this would mean death right now. However, I also want to avoid any stretching caused by the seedlings moving toward the lights from afar. It is a balancing act; one that you will develop a feel for with each successive grow. Trust your gut but be observant, so if you make a mistake, you don't repeat it needlessly in the future.

The Kush clones look fine, though there is a bit of yellowing and necrosis now. This is normal – until the plants develop root systems, they will feed off the lower leaves. These can eventually be culled. The point is to nurse the plant as a whole to viability – the individual leaves can be sacrificed to reach this goal. Based on my experience to date, these are likely to be at least a week and a half away from being transplanted into pots and moved closer to the lights.

Day 8

The Kush clones continue to grow at a good pace. I had to shimmy them left under the lights again. This is as far as I can go in this direction. Tomorrow, the lights will need to be lifted on one side or both using the chains. I try to delay this until the last possible moment because the T5s are plenty bright enough to give me a good harvest, but at a cost – and that cost is, at times, a labor-intensive daily movement of the lights. But, for me, and I'd argue for most novice growers, this bother outweighs the added cost, potential danger, and room requirements of more powerful lights. In any case, daily observation of your plants is a

Note how different twins can be. These Master Kush originated from the same mother, but one is short and bush-like while the other is taller and thin. Grow conditions and differences in topping and so on can cause big differences.

The same two plants: one a little stressed, the other not. A little TLC is in order.

Before and after. Once the new seedling breaks the soil, initial growth can be explosive.

good habit to get into. Also, happily, the growth will be explosive in the next few weeks, requiring much more movement and therefore effort on my part. But, about halfway through the bud cycle, the plants will stop adding vertical height and instead put all their resources into bud development, so this is a temporary inconvenience.

Everything in the veg room will stay as it is today. Happily, the seedlings haven't grown overnight. Normally, this wouldn't be good news, but since I wanted to arrest any potential stretching, this is just what I was hoping to see. The best news is that the fourth seed has just barely emerged from the soil. We have liftoff! Now, we'll see if it can catch its siblings in the coming days.

Day 9

This is the first day that the seedlings have shown the development of true marijuana-type leaves. They are well on their way now to becoming viable plants in their own right. Even now, the shell casing persists on the one Tangerine Dream seedling, but I leave it be. Each plant now ranges from just one and a quarter inches to just shy of two inches. The 'late' Tangerine is only a quarter inch tall.

The leaves on the Kush cuttings have begun to yellow noticeably. Don't panic when this happens on your own clones, when you get there.

One sign of maturity: emerging bud sites.

Another: white hairs emerging at calyxes. This is the best proof of female sex in cannabis.

It is totally normal. The key is that the stems are strong and the leaves are not wilting – wilting leaves are signs of impending death. Keep in mind this analogy: the cuttings are like someone on a diet; cut off from food (by lack of roots) they cannibalize themselves slowly, just as a human body on a starvation diet will begin to consume stored body fat. Unlike a human, you can't really feed the cuttings. Just try to keep their conditions stable and let them take care of generating roots – their 'mouths.' Then the watering and nutrient feeding can begin anew.

Over in the bud room, I'm now faced with a common challenge for small grows: managing uneven growth between plants. The Kush plants, which I've begun to refer to simply as Thin (slender and less de-veloped at the bottom) and Thick (shorter, more squat with several bushy stems), require that I tilt the lights at a bit of an extreme angle. Provided you set up your lights with hooks and chains that are well an-chored, this isn't dangerous, and allows the gardener to maximize light exposure. The other solution is to use a low shelf of boards to raise the shorter plant to the height of its taller sister(s). For now, I've opted for the former.

A week after moving the Kushes into flower, they are 13.5 inches and a foot tall, respectively (Thin and Thick). Based on previous grows, I expect that these plants will top out at somewhere in the area of two feet tall each, and that this growth will conclude by approximately Day 30 after moving to the 12/12 light cycle. However, this is just an estimate. Two factors may affect their final height. First, I topped these plants not once but several times as I waited for the last crop to finish up in a packed bud room. With any luck, this delayed harvest will be a larger one. The plants may, however, be shorter as a result. Secondly, this grow is occurring as we move deeper into autumn and because the grow room is located in a basement in an old house that isn't properly insulated, cooler temperatures could slow or even stunt growth. This is my first fall/winter in this particular grow room, so it's a bit of a wait and see.

Day 10

Today I start by moving the lights up (two chinks on the chain) on the left side. As I observed yesterday, this is for balance and because I ended up out late last night with friends and didn't get home until well into the night. The result: a leaf on the top of the Thin Kush got pretty badly burnt. At this stage in the plant's development, this isn't a major issue. If bud had been present, however, this would have been a costly miscalculation. In the case of bud being present, I would probably have moved the lights higher earlier. Always consider where your plants are in their growth cycle, and where you are in terms of social plans!

One nice sign is that only a shade over a week since switching these Master Kush to the 12/12 light cycle, they are already showing the white hair-like pistils that indicate their sex as female. Sex wasn't in doubt as these are clones, but it is a sign that budding is not far away now. In the case of unsexed plants (grown from seed, not clone) I would have needed to be much more vigilant in looking for signs of any interloping males amongst the female plants. The hairs are evident on multiple calyxes (the 'split' point where new stems branch out from the main stems). This is a

Tilt lights to accommodate plants of different heights. The goal is to maximize light exposure via close proximity to the T5s.

positive sign for your final harvest size as bud develops mainly at the calyx points. Before moving plants from veg to bud rooms, I ensure that an ample number of calyxes have developed. This is a sign of sexual maturity. It also signals a readiness for budding. These two are looking good.

In any case, Master Kush is an indica-dominant strain, which means they tend to develop more quickly indoors, typically three months from start to harvest in optimum conditions. This early demonstration of sex is typical of this strain, and it's one reason why I love it. Master Kush is also commonly thought to be a hardy strain, good for beginners, and it yields a nearly tasteless and potent bud. You may want to start with it if you can access Master Kush seeds.

I split a small amount (less than a quart) of water I had left over from last night between the two plants and let them be.

I water the plants in the veg room liberally as well. The seedlings in particular are drying out daily because of their close proximity to the lights. More than a day of really dry soil can kill seedlings, so I stay on top of this until the plants are moved far enough from the lights to slow

The smooth cotyledon seed leaves are now overtaken by larger leaves with more characteristic cannabis ridges.

evaporation. On the other hand, too much water can literally drown small seedlings and can lead to a destructive condition called "root rot". More benign but still problematic, this condition occurs when soil isn't allowed to dry out somewhat between waterings and then stunts root growth, as the roots don't need to stretch to grow in search of new water in waterlogged soil. Be careful, but don't overthink it – experiment with your own grow situation, write the changes in your journal, especially any changes to your water schedule over time, and tweak your routine accordingly. Greg Green's formula is: day 1 – water; days 2 and 3 – no water; day 4 – water; and so on (with feeding nutrients worked in as well). However, take the example of my grow: at the height of summer heat, if I fail to water plants daily, I risk serious harm. In fact, I nearly lost the Kush Mother by skipping one night and returning the next day to find a withered plant that took several days of heavy watering to return to normal health. The bottom line is this: let soil dry or get dry-ish before watering again in most circumstances (unless, for instance, you need to flush or water early because of non-garden related plans) but when dry,

Unless they show obvious signs of distress, clones that have begun to grow should no longer require spritzing.

give your plants some water – whatever the calendar says!

I also spritzed the leaves of the seedlings today, something that, in retrospect, isn't too smart. Though these weren't negatively affected, spritzing the leaves of these small plants could have caused burns. Moreover, these plants have root systems, so there isn't much to gain from soaking the leaves – if anything, it could slow down root development, which is counterproductive. As a rule, spritzing should only be for fresh cuttings, and only for the first few days provided they are kept in a humid environment.

Day 11

Today I fed the mature plants. Given that the Master Kushes experienced some visible stress last week from which they have happily recovered, I will go slowly in terms of ramping up the feed schedule. On that rationale, I fed the plants on the Transition feed a second time and

General Hydroponics produces a series of basic nutrients with an easy to follow feeding schedule.

will move to Bloom on the next feed. With respect to nutrients, keep this in mind: less is almost always more. A regular feed schedule of nutes is in my view a must, since they definitely boost yields and can be flushed from plants prior to harvest in any case. They are an easy way of ensuring that plants get what they need to thrive and can avoid dangerous nutrient deficiencies. Unless you plan to have an "organic" garden and rely on natural sources of nutrients such as seaweed and bat guano (products that will generally be harder to source, harder to use, and may lead to larger incurred expenses, in addition to potential problems like smell) they are a must for your grow.

So if a little is good, then why isn't a lot better? Well, while it can occasionally be worth your while to 'push' nutrients – for instance, to boost bud growth – nutrients can also burn or even kill your plants if overdosed. All nutrients will include specific directions for mix ratios with water. Follow them! Never feed your plants nutrients directly, without water. Plants will be happiest when fed a diluted, well-stirred mixture.

Also, keep in mind that nutrients are big business. The companies

A range of cut heights in these clones but they all look healthy.

These can be planted: there is clear evidence of new growth at the tops of these clones.

that sell them want you to use lots and lots – as much as possible so that you'll buy more and pad their bottom line. But your bottom line is that plants can flourish in nature without such interventions. The cannabis plant is built to survive – it ain't called "weed" for nothing! Add nutrients to your gardening routine, but don't exceed the recommended mix ratios and don't feed too frequently. In the case of an overfeed, flush the soil by running clean water through it, and use a soil flush additive if you have one on hand – also a good purchase to make. You will have to experiment with a frequency that works for you given your chosen strains and the particulars of your grow situation. Do some research online when you start growing to find out how particular strains respond to nutrients, and whether they tend to benefit from more or less than average.

In general terms, the more often your garden requires water, the more often it will require feeding. To take my garden as an example: in warmer weather, frequently I must water almost daily. In this situation,

This is typical of a weekly cull from my Kush Mother. Be sure to thin your Mother regularly to keep it healthy.

I feed twice weekly on average. Again, there isn't a one-size-fits-all formula: experiment and determine what works for you. Conversely, in the colder winter months, when I slow my watering down to every second, third or even fourth day, and slow my feeding to weekly. A helpful tip: stick to a routine as much as possible. In the summer I try to feed Tuesdays and Fridays, and Fridays only in the winter. I only divert from this if the plants look deprived like they need an early feed, or if they appear overfed. With a commitment to observation and mindfulness with respect to caring for your plants, you'll develop a gut feeling for such situations. I like Friday nights because it is the end of my (non-gardening) workweek and I like to unwind at home in the garden with a beer and commit an hour or more to care for the plants, feeding, and journaling. It really is relaxing. The routine goes a long way to minimizing mistakes. Consider a regular time that works for you, if possible.

Seedlings don't need much in the way of nutrients for the first couple of weeks and the clones don't get fed until they have started developing root balls. Mother Kush looks quite healthy today with the

Step-by-Step: Guide to Feeding Vegetative Plants

1. Draw as much water as necessary into bucket.

2. Carefully measure nutrients according to feeding schedule.

3. Stir nutrients well. Do not premix nutrients.

4. Agitate soil and remove any dead leaves.

5. Pour slowly. Don't pour so fast that water hits low leaves.

6. Allow 10-15% overflow into pans.

feed and with me having culled a number of yellowing leaves yesterday. Mother plants typically require less active care than plants being brought to harvest, at any stage of the process. Should you choose to keep one or more Mother plants, all that is really required is to trim and manicure them occasionally to maintain their size. At least once or twice a week, you should also cull dying leaves. Regular watering

Feeding Plants

1. Make sure your feed bucket is clean before starting. If feeding veg/bud nutrient solutions back-to-back (as frequently is the case) then you don't want to "contaminate" one feed with the nutrient mix from the other feed.

2. Measure cool to lukewarm water into the bucket (cold water can shock plants). Follow nutrient instructions for appropriate proportion of water to nutrients.

3. Carefully measure nutrients into water. Stir well. Be sure to shake bottles that require mixing thoroughly. Never over-pour! If in doubt, it is better to give fewer nutrients than required than to burn plants with a heavy pour.

4. If you require less than the amount of water indicated, adjust nutrient measurements proportionally (e.g. a typical nutrient schedule may be based on a mixture into four liters of water. If you require less than this, reduce nutes in direct proportion to water. Example: 2 L water = 50% of required nutrients; 8 L = double nutrients).

5. Particularly when soil is very dry (a sure sign: soil has moved away from the edges of the pots), pour slowly. Add water slowly so that it can be absorbed rather than running into the pan.

6. Avoid pouring so much that water reaches low hanging leaves.

7. Stop when soil is saturated or water begins running into pan.

8. Watering schedule will vary based on (a) proximity to lights (close = more frequent, far = less), (b) maturity of the plant being watered (mature/large = more frequent, smaller plants = less), and (c) grow room temperature and humidity (warm rooms require more frequent watering, cooler rooms, less), including proximity to fans (note that plants which are placed closer to fans may require more water than plants which are further away). In general, expect to water as frequently as daily to only every third or even fourth day.

9. Moderation is key: neither overwater plants nor allow them to dry out. Both are bad news for the health of cannabis plants. If a plant's soil has been waterlogged, allowing soil to dry out fully before re-watering can increase growth and overall plant health.

These seedlings are pretty. But they're also a bit more work since they aren't sexed like clones.

is of course a must, as is a regular feeding. For a plant that is being maintained as a Mother for more than a few months, it is also advisable to flush the soil monthly – but more on this later. Beyond the space that is required to keep a Mother plant, there really isn't much bother or cost.

Keeping a Mother has several benefits that suggest themselves. Foremost is that having a Mother plant that has been sexed grants a gardener one hundred percent certainty that clones will be female. This removes any worry of contaminating females you are bringing to bud with males – a situation that will reduce your garden to garbage. This is nothing to do with feminism or grrrl power, but cultivating cannabis is strictly a female-only endeavor. That is unless, of course, a gardener decides to breed or crossbreed plants. This can be a diverting hobby, but for most novice growers, it is a few years away at least. For most small grows, a routine that relies on clones rather than seed removes the worry and time required to sex plants. Also, maintaining a healthy Mother will save you money – clones are free whereas even a small number of seeds

Step-by-Step: Guide to Feeding Flowering Plants

1. Shake nutes as required.

2. Measure carefully. Don't over feed!

3. Stir. Be sure not to confuse with veg feed if doing simultaneously.

4. Pour slowly so dirty water doesn't hit low bud!

5. Be sure plants are on the same feeding schedule if in the same pan.

can cost well over a hundred dollars. Finally, provided you grow and select a healthy plant to turn into your Mother (you should really choose
the strongest, best looking of the bunch in your first grow to start a
Mother straight away, once sex has been determined), you improve your
chances of good yields. Clones will, after all, only be as healthy as their
parent plant.

The other option with respect to Mother plants is to 'turn over'
Mothers on a regular basis. That is, rather than keeping a Mother plant
suspended in a vegetative state for many months or years, you may decide to vegetate a sexed plant sufficiently to produce several high quality clones, then cycle it into the bud room so that it can be brought to
flower. In this case, the best of the clones taken becomes the new
Mother and the process is repeated. Using this model, you can increase
the number of plants you will harvest. Less space is required here than
when keeping a mature Mother, something that is advantageous if your
grow situation is cramped or if you wish to cultivate multiple strains in
a limited amount of space. A word of caution though: don't attempt
this until you have mastered your cloning method. The danger of this
turnover method is that if the clones die for some reason while the (now
former) Mother is brought to maturity and harvest, you could potentially exhaust your supply of plants and have to restart from seed.
Cloning from budding plants is a possible but dangerous endeavor. This
is both costly and time consuming. Err on the side of caution and keep
a healthy, happy Mother until you've become comfortable with your
gardening skills.

Otherwise, the plants look good today. The clones are healthy and,
upon inspection, the pods holding the seedlings have shown the first
signs of roots poking through the holes at the bottom of the pods. This
is great; they are nearly ready for transplant to larger pots.

The pods themselves were bone dry due to the close proximity to
the heat thrown by the lights. Beyond giving them a good soaking with
demineralized water, I also decide to pour some water into a pan so that
the plants can access water as the soil dries. Casual water in the pans,
while generally not a great idea, is a good insurance against plants drying out in hot conditions, or when required because you cannot make a
regularly scheduled watering due to out-of-garden commitments.

This monster desperately needs a haircut. Very little light is penetrating into the middle or bottom of this plant.

Day 12

This was a very quiet day. No need to move lights or plants, or to water any plants at all. That's not to say things were completely uneventful. When I entered the grow room today, the lights in the bud room, which should have been lit, remained off. After some initial confusion – everything else was working normally and there was no obvious source of a problem – it dawned on me: the timers that control the lights were off by an hour because of the overnight change from Daylight Savings to Standard time; the clocks had fallen back but I neglected to reset the timers! Not a big deal, but a reminder to check your timers periodically as a failure to change the time, while it wouldn't affect the garden, could cost you more money if you live in a jurisdiction where time-of-day charges for electricity apply.

One other quick tip that might save you some heartache down the road: save all your instructions. It's easy to toss out instructions for a timer or timed power bar. You don't want to try resetting the time or programming a schedule without the instructions on hand – or you'll need marijuana, if only to cope with the frustration. Without instructions, small appliances can be worthless, or at least require a time consuming internet search to locate the details. Save yourself some time: put them somewhere easily accessible. I keep mine right beside the timer and timed power bar I use, even if I only need to access them a couple times a year. I even saved a set of instructions I ripped apart when removing it from 'child proof' (and evidently gardener proof) packaging. But it is a good reminder that duct tape has so many uses in a home garden situation – even taping up instructions!

The alternative to keeping a mother or regularly turning over clones? Starting from scratch.

The other check I do today is temperature. As the weather outside is cooling down, I've noticed that my grow room is cooling down as well. I've hung a thermometer in the main room, away from the lights. Yesterday, the temperature in the dark showed 60°F (15.5°C). This is about ten degrees lower than optimum temperature for the grow rooms. Less than this could stunt growth, and a drop another ten or more degrees could actually harm the plants. Similarly, too hot is not good either; 80°F (27°C) requires more watering and fans to cool the room. Another ten degrees or more can harm the plants. Like Goldilocks, we're aiming for not too hot or cold, but rather, just right – a bit warmer than room temperature.

Curious about the difference under the lights, I put the thermometer in the bud room last night, about a foot away from the lights. The temperature shows today as 69°F (21°C) – well into the comfortable range. So I close up shop for the night.

Day 13

Almost two weeks in now, I started today by taking stock of the plants: the two Kushes in the bud room are 16 and 13 inches tall, and 14 and 12 inches wide respectively. The Thick Kush has ten main colas developing bud, six of which are large. Thin Kush has just eight but five of these are large and one in particular is a super cola. These are shaping up to be able to provide a good harvest. Based on my estimate from previous grows of Master Kush, these plants will need approximately 60 days in the bud room from transfer in to harvest, so these two have a little over six weeks until being done. I'm positive that these plants are about to hit maturity because not only are there the first emerging signs of actual bud formations now, but I can for the first time detect the sweet smell of marijuana when I handle the plants, something I will try to do as little as possible so that I minimize disruption of the THC-laden bud.

There wasn't any need to water either plant today as there was still some water in each pan and the soil in each pot is still moist. There were some minor burns on the tips of some upper fan leaves on each plant. Such burns, caused by the plants growing too close to the lights, aren't a major concern provided they are minor and don't recur. I nip a couple of the burnt tips off with my fingers to allow the leaves to continue to grow; burns created either by heat or chemicals which are left unattended

Adjusting Lights

1. Adjust lights on chain with hooks to achieve optimum distance between plants and T5 fluorescents. Note that you will have to keep watching and adjusting plants until approximately the end of the third week in flowering, at which time vertical growth will cease and the plants will dedicate themselves to bud growth.

2. If minor burns occur, trim plants of dead material as needed.

3. Strike a balance between the danger of burning plants (if they hit the T5s) versus keeping tops so far away that they stretch and have reduced yields due to lack of proximity to T5s. Close proximity is particularly important given the relatively lower lumen output of T5s versus other higher discharge lighting options.

4. It is vital to ensure that lights are free of all impediments for safety reasons. Lights must not touch anything, and power cords must never be left hanging where they might be exposed to moisture.

5. If plants grow to the point that lights are at their maximum height for your grow space, you will have to train stems down to keep them under lights.

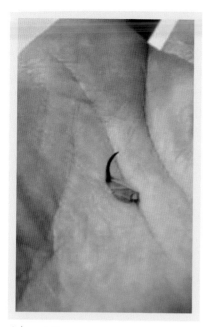

A burnt tip.

Trim any dead material from plants burnt by lights.

Repeated topping has produced multiple stems for more bud sites.

Space between stems is a must for light penetration. Trim centres of plants as needed.

An old Mother can grow quite thick in the main stem. The top canopy is stealing all the light from lower branches. Lower T5 wattage means you should keep small Mothers that are much better trimmed than this beast.

will tend to turn leaves slowly necrotic. It is better to trim them, even roughly as I have today, and save the leaves for continued growth.

I also move the lights up on their chain, two chinks on the right, one on the left. This gives the plants a bit more breathing room. I will, however, need to be vigilant in the coming three weeks. This is prime time for the main explosion of growth that generally starts about ten days to two weeks after plants are moved into the 12/12 light cycle. It isn't uncommon for plants to as much as double in height in a couple weeks, all while adding the major bud formations. During this time, while you will want to keep the lights as close as possible to maximize the opportunity for both calyx growth and bud development, it is important also to check the plants daily, preferably soon after the lights have turned on for the day (or night, as mine are set up to operate). It is an exciting time in any case, and is quite interesting to track the growth day-to-day. In the case that you are unavailable to tend to your garden in a timely manner, err on the side of caution: move the lights up and further

| Staggered calyxes: evidence that care was taken to avoid stretching. There are many sites for bud formation. | The gentle sway of a stem that has been super cropped. What doesn't kill it makes pot stronger! |

away from the plant tops, even if only for a single evening when you have plans. Since the main or "terminal" cola will be the highest point on each plant, the most valuable site for bud production will be closest to the lights. Be careful!

The clones and Mother Kush need little care today. The seedlings are just over two inches tall. Though there is little visible to distinguish between the Tangerine Dream and Pandora seedlings in terms of the leaf shape and size, there are minor differences in height between the plants. Such minor differences are normal – no matter how hard you work to create good garden conditions, genetics will determine how the plants develop, at least to some extent. Your job is merely to provide the best possible circumstances for those genetics to flourish. However, one frequent cause for height differences between plants of the same strain is that males, as with humans, tend to be taller on average than females. When growing from seed, I take note of taller seedlings as ones more likely to be male. This doesn't always follow, but it does allow you to 'cheat' a bit when looking for males (down the road, when brought to maturity under the 12/12 light cycle) when checking by naked eye. I'm hopeful that most of these will be female as these seeds are feminized – my first attempt with feminized seeds. But males are still possible. When I grew the Master Kush from seed, from non-feminized seeds, I averaged slightly better than 50% female to male. It will be interesting to see how these mature. Even 75% would be a great result.

Day 14

No noticeable action in the bud room today. Though a small amount of water remains in each pan, the soil itself is fairly dry in each pot so I give each plant a small amount of water. Otherwise, everything looks good.

I also water the Kush Mother and seedlings, the latter of which are now starting to look like real plants. I do a bit more of an invasive check

During the first weeks in the flowering light cycle, plants grow explosively, as much as doubling in size.

Clones (left) and seedlings (right) that are the same age to the day. Two weeks on, clones look more impressive. But seedlings are closing fast.

of clones. Because I clone in soil, it can be difficult to tell when the roots are developed sufficiently to transplant into proper pots. The easiest way to tell is by sight. If roots protrude from the holes in the bottom of the pods, the clones are good to go. However, this doesn't always happen. Another good measure is the calendar. Typically, my clones are ready to transplant in no less than two weeks, no more than three. A third way is to judge by new growth. The development of new leaf structures, no matter how small, is evidence that roots have taken hold. Only plants with a working root structure will engage in new growth. These don't have evidence of this yet. This leaves a final tactic: gently moving the soil away from the base of the stem to look for root development. This is invasive, so you should try to do this rarely and only once before planting, lest you damage the clones. That said, I've done this in the past without compromising the clones. So, if in doubt, you can do this. I complete a quick check of mine today – one has just an emerging root, less than 1/4 inch in length. The other is twice as long. I decide to give them a few more days before moving.

Burned, but by a different flame. The burnt edges of this fan leaf are more typical of a nutrient than lamp burn. Slow down on the nutes!

Day 15

I feed the Kush again today, moving to the Bloom formulation. This is a bit earlier than I otherwise might, but the plants – which I inadvertently fed a bit too much last time – responded quite well. Noting the healthy response, I decide to speed up the feed to spark growth. There are a couple of lessons learned here: first, only by observing and journaling was I able to determine that the plants benefitted and clearly needed nutrients to be stepped up. Second, nothing focuses the mind like a mistake. Though I over-poured the Flora Nova Boom last week, I am bang on tonight. It is easy to get comfortable and make a goof; this happy error was a good reminder for me to pay attention rather than gardening on cruise control.

I also had to move the lights up two chinks. By next week, I will need to move the chains up to the upper hook, the highest I can move them. Despite taking action to prevent burns the taller, thin Kush top cola leaves were slightly burned today. The explosive growth phase has truly begun.

Over in the veg room, the clones aren't any worse for wear after my little peek yesterday. Now that I know that there are some roots, I move the clones up with the seedlings, much closer to the lights. This should spark growth, something that would have been dangerous to the clones when lacking roots (clones lacking roots can be hydrated sufficiently to stand the warmer temps that accompany closer proximity to the lights).

Day 16

No need to water in the bud room today, though I did shimmy the two plants to the left, the side where the lights are slightly higher. This is a good time saver, an alternative to changing the light setup itself. That said, it is a short-term solution; I will need to move the lights up tomorrow or the next day to be sure.

Also important with respect to lights is the actual light distribution the plants received. Today, I observed that the plants were bent slightly toward the lights. To counter this, I spun the pots 180 degrees. Over the next day or so, the plants will 'correct' themselves and grow more vertically. This isn't necessary to do every day, but if you don't turn your pots to allow for uneven light distribution at least once or twice a week, you can end up with plants that are twisted oddly. In some cases, this can be beneficial due to space constrictions, but more often it is not. Most important is to allow all parts of the plants good access to light. The result of failing to do this is retarded bud developments on calyx formations that have been light deprived.

The Kush seem to have grown markedly in the last few days, so I decide to check against the measurements from three days ago. As I suspected, each plant is more than two inches taller and the same in width. Both plants have accelerated bud formation on the upper cola. Even in the lower reaches of each plant, buds are forming. Lots of white hairs are growing in these areas. They develop a look like very thin, white pasta-type formations. This is a sign of healthy development, and a confirmation of female sex in cases where the plants' sex is not known prior to budding.

In the veg room, I note today that the seedlings, which I water heavily as their pods are dry, have largely caught up to the clones in terms of overall size. This is typical. Since the clones should have more mature root development inside the next week, I expect that the clones and seedlings will roughly match each other's growth through the rest of the vegetative state.

I check for roots protruding from the pods of either plant but no luck. I do have a false alarm; what looks like a white root is actually a bit of

Sexing Plants

1. For plants that are grown from germinated seeds rather than established female clones, you will have to be vigilant about sexing once plants are moved from vegetative growth to budding. There is no danger of contamination by males while in vegetative growth (think of vegging plants as being "pre-puberty").

2. Plants will begin to show initial signs of sex as early as a few days after being placed in the 12/12 light cycle, and certainly initial signs should be visible to the naked eye within a week.

3. It may take two weeks or longer before you can definitively sex plants. Be sure to watch for hermies (plants that have male and female sex characteristics). These should be treated as males and eliminated from your garden.

4. To sex plants, observe calyxes, the junctions between the main stem(s) and branches. Females will typically sprout white-ish hair-like follicles. Males will have bunches of round pods that literally look like balls. These balls will grow in round bunches and are difficult to miss.

5. Once these burst, females will be fertilized, reducing your harvest. Even one male will wreck a crop - err on the side of caution and remove any potential males before pollination (you will have, on average, a week between the first sign of male sex characteristics and danger).

6. Plants can potentially be sexed early using a microscope, but you generally will have enough play, time-wise, to sex plants by the naked eye.

7. Male plants, once identified, should be removed from the garden, destroyed, and bagged. Do not leave male plants exposed if they have seed pods that might be released.

8. You will learn by trial and, unfortunately, error. Once females have been affected by males, it is better to start from scratch. Don't be greedy; it is better to eliminate one male, even a potential one, pre-emptively and be wrong, than to lose half a dozen female plants.

9. Remember that once plants are sexed as female, they may be cloned in perpetuity. Sexing is only something you should have to do when introducing new strains to your garden.

Early bud formations. Note the hair-like formations at the calyxes and the absence of "balls." Master Kushes are more green than other strains in this area.

the soil mix. It is easy to make mistakes in terms of "finding what you are looking for" when cloning and sexing plants. It is best to double and triple check, particularly in the case of sexing, rather than jumping to potentially costly conclusions.

Day 17

Success! Today there is clear evidence of a root protruding from the pod of one of the clones. This is my signal to transplant out of the pods and into one-gallon pots. It isn't the end of the world if you fail to transplant immediately in such cases, though it can potentially stunt plant development if the root ball doesn't have sufficient room to expand. As with most aspects of maintaining a daily garden, there are different of schools of thought on this issue. Some gardeners prefer smaller pots, bringing "bonsai" style plants through a full harvest cycle in small, root-packed pots. Others opt for much larger pots. Don't overthink it: experiment,

Step-by-Step: Transplanting Seedlings and Clones to Medium Pots

1. Line pot bottoms with newspaper.

2. Fill with soil and pre-moisten. Labels pots in advance.

3. Transfer clone/seedling, keeping tiny rootball intact.

4. Trim dying/low-hanging fan leaves as required.

5. *Remove all dead leaves. Tamp plant into soil.*

6. *Ensure plant is secure in soil and clear of pot edges.*

7. *Water and place under lights.*

Roots sticking out of seed pots: a sure sign a transplant is needed.

Careful with autoflowers: small pots can force early budding. Bigger pots are better for these.

record results over successive generations of plants and develop a system that works for you.

In today's transplant, I observe that all the clones and seedlings have healthy root formations. The clones' roots are slightly larger and more developed. Some of the lower fan leaves on the clones are yellowing and necrotic. This is normal as the plants have fed on these while their root systems developed. Now that they are more mature plants in their own right, I trim these to promote overall healthy growth for these plants, so that they can focus on new healthy stem and leaf growth rather than being held back by compromised leaves. The clone whose roots I disturbed for a peek a couple of days ago exhibits some weird, white-ish necrotic looking material on the upper leaf. This could be a coincidence, or it could be the result of my stressing the plant. I'm not too worried, but in such cases you are best advised to keep a close eye on affected plants until any observed symptoms pass and they return to a look of full health. I trim the leaf and will watch for similar symptoms making an appearance.

When successfully transplanted, snug those vegging plants up close to the T5s to spur growth.

I make another small error: with one of the Tangerine seedlings, rather than easing it out of the soil by massaging the pod and tapping it out, I instinctually pull it by the stem. This may be a good strategy for harvesting root vegetables like carrots, but it sucks if your intent is to minimize disruption of a fragile cannabis root system. I have effectively ripped apart the lower root structure of the one seedling. Hopefully, this won't have too profound an impact on its development. Word to the wise: be self-aware when working in your garden. It is all too easy to make small but costly mistakes through simple neglect, excitement, or absentmindedness.

The Pandora at first appears a bit wilted, but on closer inspection, this is perhaps more a strain difference between it and the Tangerine Dream. The latter are already taking on a slightly more robust, full shape. I'm gratified to see that the seedling that was planted several days later than the others has essentially caught up. There is little to distinguish it from the other Tangerines. This is a plus since plants that are growing at much different rates can pose a challenge in terms of organizing the room so that all plants enjoy a close proximity to the lights.

A somewhat thinned Mother. Smaller would be easier to manage.

It isn't unusual for one plant to outgrow its sisters. This is the big growth spurt: as much as four inches growth in a day or so.

Seed leaves about to drop.

Day 18

I watered each of the Master Kush plants with half a liter of water today. Growth and budding continues rapidly. As a result, I was forced to move the lights up on the left again. I am nearly at the end of my chain (though thankfully not my rope – everything is proceeding nicely now).

In the veg room, the Mother Kush continues to look good. I water it with 1.5 liters and look for any dead leaves; there are only a couple. The cotyledons on the seedlings are yellowed now and look like they will fall off directly. Otherwise, the baby plants all look quite good. I finish my bottle of distilled water today and will switch these to tap water for their next watering. This is fine as they are now basically out of their most fragile developmental stage. Observation of the Kush clone that had strange white marking shows what might be a minor amount of white on an upper leaf. Otherwise, it looks fine. I will continue to monitor closely.

Day 19

Things continue to develop nicely in the bud room today. The Kush plants have nice bud development and a plethora of large, healthy fan leaves. They are, however, growing more and more unbalanced in terms of height. I adjust the lights by moving the right chain up. I don't really have a choice about this since Thin Kush would likely hit the lights overnight if I don't. However, Thick Kush is now more substantially removed from the lights. I've decided that this is okay for now, but suspect that in the next couple days I will need to move it into its own pan and raise it toward the lights with boards so that it enjoys the same amount of light as its sister.

In the veg room, the fetal leaves on the Pandora and Tangerine Dream are very yellow and about to fall off. I'm going to give the seedlings their first feed once this happens. This is the marijuana equivalent of a rite of passage: loss of cotyledons marking the move from childhood to adolescence. These plants are about ready for a more adult, if initially heavily diluted, feeding schedule.

The Master Kush grown from clones look good. Though they have yet to show any clear vertical growth, the leaves for the most part remain green and lush. This is the case for two of the three at least; the weak sister has some necrosis across the top leaf structure. I have a theory here: since this plant was taller than its two sisters, this could simply be a case of the leaves being less equipped than necessary for such close proximity to the lights in its early life cycle. I cut the top of this whole structure. This has two benefits. Firstly, it brings it more closely into line with the size of its two sister plants, which will ease lighting. Second, I

Houston, we have a problem. These leaves show advancing necrosis. Better to trim compromised areas than lose the whole plant.

will now monitor this plant for any new necrosis. If it develops along the lower reaches of the plant I will likely ditch it and start a new clone. Discretion truly can be the better part of valor: you may decide that it's better to retire a sick plant in favor of a more robust new plant. On the other hand, it can be an interesting challenge to attempt to nurse a compromised plant back to health, provided it does not turn into a threat in terms of communicating whatever problems it might have to its neighbors. This is really a judgment call. I like the challenge of saving sick plants. Marijuana is called "weed" after all – they can be surprisingly hard to kill through neglect. In any case, the choice is yours.

Day 20

Today, I decide to split up the two budding Kush. I move Thin Kush to the left and, in its own pan, Thick Kush to the furthest right I can along the light. Both are now more snug up close to the lights. This is a good

Thin Kush is taller and is at the higher side of the fluorescent light while Thick Kush is shorter and is at the lower side. This allows both plants to be close to the light.

call because the top cola of each plant now show defined, if very immature, bud structures. The lower calyxes continue to sprout white pistil hairs, so they are developing as expected. You will likely note that lower branches will develop more slowly and ultimately be much reduced in size from the cola tops that are much closer to the light sources. This highlights the importance of light proximity.

I also feed all the plants today, in both rooms. Note the much darker tone of the vegetative feed, which is a product of the much higher proportion of nitrogen in these additives. I take care when feeding not to mix the two buckets, keeping each on the same side of the room as the appropriate grow room to avoid confusion. Also an important tip here: because I will be feeding the developing plants at a much diluted mixture of the same nutrients as Mama Kush, if feeding at the same time (I'm not today – still waiting for definite growth on the baby plants before their initial feed) I cap each bottle after each pour. It might seem like not a big deal to leave the bottles open between feeds but it is all too easy to clumsily kick over a bottle. At more than thirty dollars for

Mother Maintenance

1. Thin out the plant occasionally to allow lower areas to grow, at least once a month. The plant will naturally gravitate to light and grow a "canopy" across the top. Without occasional thinning it will choke off growth on lower branches.

2. Take off necrotic leaves by hand day-to-day. Mothers, once big, are resilient. Err on the side of caution and take more off, particularly if the growth is unhealthy.

3. It is not generally a serious problem (or fire hazard) if the top of one or more stems brushes lights on occasion but try to avoid this. If you are very busy or going away for several days (and leaving your garden in the care of another), top your plant one or more inches in advance.

4. Maintain your Mother through topping and/or training to achieve a size and shape that suits the needs of your grow room. Even a small plant, less than a foot tall, will be more than adequate to produce many clones on a consistent basis.

5. Feed twice weekly on average, and feed once a week with water only (to give soil a break and flush excess nutrients), more as you water more, less as you water less. Experiment with what your plants respond to best by keeping good records in your grow log.

6. Once a month, flush the Mother's soil. Use a nutrient flush agent – water alone is not sufficient to avoid "soil lock" on mature Mothers that are being fed nutrients weekly for months or even years.

7. Read the leaves! They'll tell you if you're using too many nutrients or not enough.

8. Mothers can last a long time and produce many dozen clones for cultivation and eventual harvest – take care of it and it will take care of you!

Flowering plants undergoing growth spurts need extra feedings to keep growing. Don't starve your growing plants.

some bottles of nutrients, this presents the potential for an expensive mistake. Take your time: always rebottle nutes between uses, even minutes apart. Also, be sure to mix your feed when feeding – don't pre-mix!

One bit of good news today: the Kush that had earlier shown the strange white on its leaves looks completely healthy. It has not reappeared. I'm feeling pretty confident now that this plant will be okay.

My only other bit of work today is some Mother maintenance. I tend to give my Mother a good look over when feeding. Because it has grown up into the lights, I top it in several places today. I also remove it from under the lights for a bird's eye view. This is a good strategy to employ from time to time; you'd be surprised what you might miss if you are always looking at the plants in profile. What I observe is that it has formed a nearly impenetrable canopy of healthy fan leaves. This is an encouraging sign of overall health. However, it also reduces the chance for leaves on lower branches to develop normally. I had to remove a handful of yellowed leaves. Some, with red stems, are merely at the end of their normal life cycle for a plant that has been alive for what would be the

I snipped the top off this compromised plant to give it a chance at healthy growth.

The challenge of an old Mother: topping doubles stems, creating a fan leaf wall that blots out most light to the lower branches.

Culling a big Mother can create a fair bit of trim waste.

equivalent of a full life-cycle in an outdoor setting (this plant would have surely been harvested by now if exposed to reduced daylight hours outdoors, something I have artificially avoided by keeping it in the veg room's 18/6 light/dark cycle). Others are shriveled, yellow, and underdeveloped. This is a symptom of lack of access to light. I pick all these leaves off. I also thin the upper canopy by cutting some stems out sufficiently to allow light to penetrate to the lower reaches of the plant. This is a fair bit of cutting for one day, and the Kush Mother may look a little worse for wear for a few days. Ultimately however, it will benefit from the TLC. Don't neglect your Mother plants – their continued health is the bedrock upon which your garden will grow.

Day 21

Post-feed, both plants have responded really well. There is absolutely no evidence of even the slightest chemical burns. This tells me the plants are getting the nutes they need and, if anything, might benefit from more frequent feedings. As such, I will likely feed again in three days or so and will continue to accelerate the feed schedule until such time as the plants tell me to back off with minor burns. Thick Kush has responded well to closer proximity to the lights. I need to move the lights up on the right by a couple chinks on the chain to make the Thick Kush more in line with its sister. Thick Kush now measures 19 inches high and 17 wide at its widest point. Thin Kush is slightly more than 21 inches tall and 15 wide.

I expect each should max out somewhere around two feet, a height which is just under the maximum height my bud room can accommodate. Because I moved them into the bud room at approximately ten inches each, I can make this educated guess based on experience. In previous grows, if I let these plants reach a height much greater than one foot while vegging, I risked them taking off in the bud room to a height that is taller than the lights. I try to avoid this: not only does moving them through once they reach about ten inches in height allow me to cycle the plants through more quickly (saving precious days, thus leading to more frequent harvests), but it also means I'm less likely to have to bend the tallest cola to fit under the lights. This is something

The first real bud on this Master Kush faces the T5s for max exposure. Now things get fun to watch.

Initially bud will form on the uppermost colas, but lower branches will follow shortly.

Young plants cannot handle heavy nutrient loads. Be sure to dilute first feedings according to schedule.

you can accomplish with stakes, but why create work where none need exist? Word to the wise novice gardener: be meticulous about recording measurements of particular strains of plants across multiple crops. As I've mentioned, I tend to measure weekly. But if this is too fastidious for your style, at the very least be sure to measure at two points: first when moving from veg to bud, and second when the maturing plants have reached their maximum vertical height. This will be four to five weeks after being transitioned to the 12/12 light/dark cycle. This will allow you to generalize some conclusions: eight inches in veg tends to equate to a mature height of 22 inches, ten to 25, 12 to 27, etc. It will vary, but developing the ability to predict this and to tailor your plants' development to the size of your grow room, will enable you to have a more successful and problem-free grow in future. You'll appreciate the relative predictability when this work pays off.

In the veg room, the Mother looks good and needs no care or watering. I decide to feed the small plants today, splitting two liters of the weakest concentration on the feed schedule (Seedling) between the seven plants. Note that the color of this feed is much lighter and diluted compared to the dark feed the Mother got yesterday. I will watch over the next couple days to see how the plants respond to their first nutrients.

The Pandora is now over three inches tall and five wide, whereas the three Tangerine Dream are about the same height but about an inch less wide on average. The three Kushes are each about four and a half inches tall. Two are about six inches wide each. The one I culled is only about four inches across. This is not a big deal. This plant should catch up to its sisters down the road.

Day 22

Not much action in the bud room today. I water each plant with about ½ liter of water and move the light up one chink on the right.

In the veg room, the small plants have responded without incident to their first feed. There are no burns or anything else that would indicate a negative impact. In fact, today is the first day I can observe clear evidence of new growth at the calyxes of these plants. Also, the lower fan leaves are further away from the soil, which previously they were almost brushing. Note: keep fan leaves clear of soil: they will die if they get caught in soil when watering, particularly once you start feeding, as they will then be exposed directly to the nutes. These should easily hold their own now with the plants that were grown from seed.

This plant is slender enough that light is penetrating from above.

In retrospect, this thicker Kush should have been thinned of fan leaves in the centre to allow more light to penetrate.

Can you tell which are clones and which are seedlings?

Only Pandora is noticeably larger. Not a surprise given its shorter life cycle.

In fact, I had to remove my first boards from underneath these plants today so that they are further away from the lights. This is excellent evidence of growth; we're off to the races now. All seven also needed additional water, even after yesterday's feed. Even though the first three weeks have been fairly slow, these young plants should really take off over the next couple weeks and are almost certainly more than halfway to their move into the bud room. You blink one moment and the next the kids are all grown up and moving out of the house and into the world – or, in this case, to the bud room where they will develop a nice crop of tasty bud for their patient caretakers.

Day 23:

This was a really nice, quiet day. Other than spinning all plants 180° to even out light distribution, I had nothing much to do today; there's no need for watering, light movement, or trimming. Everything looks

The first calyxes have formed. Vegetative growth is well under way.

While the highest cola is big and beautiful, large buds have begun to develop on lower branches now.

healthy. Enjoy these days – you'll never know when what you expected to be a 10-minute visit to the garden will turn into an hour or more while you solve a number of problems. Because not much is going on, I sit and look over the plants whilst enjoying a tasty beverage. I really enjoy just sitting quietly and observing the garden on nights like this. It is totally relaxing, almost like a form of meditation. Enjoy!

Day 24

There's still not much going on in the bud room. Everything looks good but beyond feeding the Kush again and moving the lights up a bit, there's not much to do.

In the veg room, I feed the Mother and top it as the canopy was brushing the lights. It is important to note that leaves brushing the fluorescent T5 bulbs from time to time don't pose much of a risk to a mature plant like the Mother. There isn't really a fire risk either; leaves that hit the lights just burn and whither.

Though growing well, these vegging plants aren't mature enough to top or super crop yet.

The young plants have really taken off now. In fact, I need to spin them daily to avoid them growing into a lean. I had to remove another board today and suspect that another will be gone tomorrow or the next day as they are growing quickly now. I also move the stunted Kush away from the others slightly as it was being overshadowed by one of its larger sisters. It's important to watch for the plants bullying one another out of light and to intervene so that smaller plants have a chance to develop; no one likes a bully! This Kush, while compromised, should turn out just fine. In fact, in line with Nietzsche's famous observation that "What doesn't kill us makes us stronger," I've noted that plants that have undergone one or another type of minor trauma while vegging or even early in the bud stage will end up stronger and with an even heavier crop when all is said and done. Don't give up on plants that have had to face a bit of adversity. Help them to reach their potential.

The 'late' Tangerine Dream that was planted a few days after the others because of the dead seed actually looks biggest and healthiest. This could mean that it is a male. However, it could just be the best one, and a candidate for saving as the Tangerine Mother. Anyway, I'll keep my eye on how these three develop in comparative terms. It's a good strategy to keep an eye out for Mother candidates early so that you save your best genetics for subsequent crops. A good Mother will give you literally dozens of plants over its life cycle. Take care in choosing it.

Day 25

Other than moving Thin Kush as far to the right as possible under the lights, not much is happening today in the bud room. In the veg room, I take advantage of the quiet day to give the Kush Mother another good cull. Basically, all I'm really worried about here is how thick the top canopy has grown. My strategy is to compare stems that have grown close together and to selectively cut out the weaker looking ones. The smaller plants are fine, though a few have the beginnings of green mossy formations along the soil tops. This isn't an imminent danger, but does signal a need to back off the watering schedule for these plants a bit. They clearly need less now that the tops of the soil are further from the lights,

Taken down a notch: the Mother's canopy is cut back several inches.

I've elected to take off quite a bit in an effort to improve light penetration.

leading to slower evaporation. Overwatering can be a problem in the sense that it can waterlog roots and the development of moss can signal the development of fungus, the latter being more dangerous or even life threatening. I respond to this by agitating the soil of the affected plants, and scraping the mossy formations off and disposing of them.

Day 26

In the bud room, the plants have reached the fullest extent of the lights. I will shortly have to move the chains onto the upper hook, something I don't always have to do. These two will evidently be on the large side. In fact, I position the terminal cola of Thin Kush strategically between two bulbs in the lights so that, in the case it has a spurt overnight, it will be less likely to hit the bulbs directly.

Not surprisingly, both Kushes now show thickening bud, and both plants are filling in the area between calyxes. They are closing in on full growth. Within a week, or two at most, vertical growth should cease and

Place plants strategically under T5s so that tall colas don't burn!

The lights can be moved closer to the top of this Kush unless vertical growth isn't finished yet.

Organize by size to maximize light exposure for plants growing at different rates. This Pandora needs to be raised toward the lights to receive the same lumens as the taller Master Kush.

TANGERINE·OCT31   TANGERINE·OCT 29   TANGERINE·OCT 27   KUSH OCT 26

Take the time to move plants around under the lights on a regular basis. You will be rewarded with more even growth and avoid stretching that will reduce yields.

bud development will slowly taper off. From there the plants will ripen over the course of three weeks or so and the fan leaves will slowly begin to wilt and die. These plants have a more pronounced odor now. Still, they have a way to go yet as there is little resin evident on the leaves and none of the bud has changed color. Lots of white hairs are still to be seen.

In the veg room today I split the developing plants into separate pans. The first is comprised of the Pandora and the larger two Kushes. The second is the runt Kush plus the three Tangerine Dreams.

Why split them up? The rationale is simple: keeping them in the same pans (and therefore at the same distance from the lights) would risk either burns for the former group or reduced light exposure for the latter. I solve the problem by removing two boards from under the first group of plants and placing the boards under the second, smaller group.

Note that there is about a two-inch disparity in height between the two groups now but that they are sitting equally close to the lights. There is another visible difference between the two groups: the smaller ones remain quite wet and I again need to scrap the soil to remove green moss. The taller group is dry and in fact requires a small watering. This is a result of different growth rates. Hopefully, now that they are up close to the lights, the smaller ones will catch up. This could, however, also be a function of the genetics of each strain. With the exception of the Kush made runty by the emergency topping, the other three

Boards under pans are a great solution to the problem of plants growing at different rates. Just be sure you create a stable base so that the plants don't fall.

Problem solved: despite the height disparities across these young plants, they are all receiving maximum exposure to the T5s.

are Tangerines. It could be that this strain grows slower, or smaller, than the Master Kush and Pandora. Given that this is my first attempt with this strain, I will journal my observations of these plants more diligently than I typically do with the Kush.

Day 27

Though there wasn't much to do tonight, I decided to move tomorrow's feed up a day – not because of any need I can see in the garden, but to account for the fact that I have dinner plans tomorrow night and likely

Thick bud growth has exploded on the Master Kush. See how developing plants with numerous, closely spaced calyxes pays off in more bud.

It's often a good idea to trim large fan leaves that block lower bud from full light exposure.

won't be back to tend to the garden until late into the night. Moreover, I may be enjoying myself and would rather avoid a more time-consuming feed when I am tired and/or properly buzzed. It's always good to plan your gardening around your social life when possible to avoid making your daily grow a chore.

I feed Mother Kush on the Aggressive Growth schedule and the smaller plants on the Growth schedule. I decide against moving any plants but I do want to maximize their exposure. I'll likely move them down tomorrow.

Light deficits can also be the cause of discolored fan leaves: the large fan leaves of this Master Kush could be trimmed significantly to allow light penetration into lower levels of the plants.

Discolored fan leaves in the early stages of flowering can be a sign of nutrient deficiency or overfeeding.

Day 28

Returning from my late dinner, I note that the two Master Kushes have a small number of necrotic leaves for the first time since they were transitioned to the 12/12 light cycle. This is most likely due to minor chemical burns from the accelerated feed. It is far too early for either plant to be shedding leaves as part of the ripening process. It isn't the end of the world. This may seem callous, but I'm not hurting the plants intentionally. They will be fine and, in fact, have only about five weeks of life remaining. My goal is to maximize their bud load and this means playing with the nutrients. It is good to know that I've finally brought the plants up against their nutrient-load limit. I will back off any further acceleration now. I nip off the affected leaves to minimize stress on the plants.

The bud on each plant continues to thicken and fill in continuously along the stems with fewer gaps. The stems all look strong and still have the ability to support the bud now weighing them down. I don't need to stake these yet. Thin Kush is now fully two feet tall and Thick

Note the bud developments beginning to overwhelm the leaves and stems. Soon, the sugar leaves and other areas around the bud will be covered with sticky, THC-laden resin. For many strains, it isn't unusual to see a continuous line of thick bud rather than delineated bud formations.

Kush is twenty inches. They look fantastic and are likely close to maximum vertical growth. It will be fun to watch them mature and ripen over the coming weeks.

The plants in the veg room are also enjoying a blast of growth. They are in their main vegetative growth phase. The Pandora and two Kush are six inches tall, with the Tangerines and outlier Kush each pushing closer to four inches tall. I take a day off from watering, though arguably the larger group could use it. Still, better to risk one dry night to promote root development.

As it turns out, I did goof a bit on the lights for this group. A couple of the uppermost Kush fan leaves are burnt, though not seriously. I nip the ends with my fingers and remove enough boards to keep all the plants a safe but efficient distance from the lights.

The Mother didn't need much care today, though I did decide to cull the sides for horizontal growth a bit, having culled for vertical growth earlier this week. It is important to keep the Mother in check in both directions.

These vegging Tangerine Dreams are almost tall enough to top for the first time. Topping is a key strategy for increasing yields, despite the added growth times required.

Day 29

I watered the Kushes in the bud room today. I used only half a liter for each, but there was still significant spillover in the pans. In retrospect, I probably could – and should – have waited another day. This was more a product of habit, watering on the summer schedule rather than late fall. Additionally, today I removed the chain from the left side of the lights altogether (the light is hanging from the lower of two hooks) and given how skewed the lights are, I will have to adjust the right side soon.

On the veg side, I watered two liters into Mother Kush. It was fine otherwise. I had to remove more boards from the younger plants. The Pandora and Kush have noticeably outpaced the Tangerines and lone Kush now. In fact, they have grown to a size where they will be ready for topping in the next few days. This will not only maximize my chances of a high yield for these plants, but will also give the slower growers a chance to catch up, if only temporarily.

It is beginning to look like the Pandora and two Master Kushes will move to the bud room ahead of their birth-mates, given that the two Kushes currently budding have the better part of a month left, and that the other room has some space restrictions. I've had a maximum of five plants in there at one time, to date, and that was a stretch – or, rather, a crush. The plants all suffered light deprivation to some extent because of the cramped quarters, with corresponding drops in their yields. A delay and second round of topping before moving these plants over won't be the end of the world. In fact, it will allow the vegging plants to mature more fully, which will increase yield size.

A few words about topping: there is no small amount of industry/on-line debate about preferred methods of maximizing yield. Nutrient use is of course one of the most basic, as I explained in my introduction about the tools and supplies that every novice gardener can't do without. But there are several direct interventions with the cannabis plants that rec-ommend themselves. The best of these, for a beginner, is topping.

Topping is perhaps the best and most accurately named activity asso-ciated with growing marijuana. There's very little mystery to it. The ra-tionale is simple: when you cut off the top of a main stem, the plants respond by growing two stems for the one whose top has been removed.

Topping

1. When to top? When plants are well into vegetative growth. They should be at least eight inches to a foot tall or more.

2. Where to top? The terminal stem but above new growth so that new stems develop quickly. Just above a calyx is best.

3. Why? Topping should increase yields by 25 to 40%.

4. Sterilize scissors before cutting if they are soiled from other tasks.

5. A large fan leaf (or two) may need to be removed as well, depending on where the cut is made. Be sure that the newly exposed sections have ad-equate access to light.

6. It is okay to top plants multiple times. However, allow time between toppings for recovery and establish-ment of new growth.

7. Don't top plants after vegetative growth is complete – definitely not after bud has started to sprout!

8. Topping is an excellent way to allow smaller plants to catch up to larger cohorts. This will help to promote a more even canopy across plants, which makes even light distribution easier to accomplish.

9. Experiment: Test by selecting two plants of the same strain. Top one only. Measure the difference in yields between plants. Continue over multiple generations.

Step-by-Step: Guide to Topping

1. Measure stems to ensure plants are tall enough to top.

2. Select the best site to make a cut.

3. Fan leaves may need to be trimmed as well.

4. New growth just above calyxes are ideal places to top young plants.

5. Topped plants can look a little bare and uneven but they recover quickly and with more robust growth.

6. Post-top: new growth has already begun here.

7. Another ideal candidate: tall and thin, this Tangerine Dream would benefit from spreading horizontally.

8. You may also decide to top more aggressively. Much more is being trimmed from this plant.

9. Note the two growth sites just underneath the cut: these will now take off with space to grow.

10. Remove trimmed tops.

11. Plants will broaden, becoming more bush-like after topping.

The Kush on the right is a prime candidate for topping. This will also allow the slightly shorter plants to the left to catch up.

You can also do this for multiple stems. I have moved from one to multiple toppings in some cases. This can both maximize yields and allow slower plants in the vegetative state to catch up. The slow plants keep their single top cola, while their generational cohorts undergo two or even three tops so that the slower companion(s) can catch up. Then they can all be moved and, ultimately, harvested at the same time. The arithmetic speaks for itself: if one stem equals a good amount of pot, two or more stems generally equates to a great amount of pot.

Before topping, a plant in the vegetative state must be sufficiently developed to withstand the stress of having its top lopped off. Typically, this means a minimum of three or even four weeks of growth. In time, you will gain a feel for when a plant is ready to be topped. I typically top mine when they are between eight and ten inches tall. The top is quite easily accomplished and is pretty difficult to screw up. Make the cut in the uppermost inch or two of the main stem or stems, ideally where there is emerging growth. This growth point will soon develop multiple new stems. You must cut the stem itself, not just fan leaves; the latter will accomplish nothing substantive. I usually leave

Super Cropping

1. Stems can be super cropped before and/or after topping. However, topping first will provide more stems that can then be super cropped.

2. Use an index finger as a support for the stem that is to be super cropped. Essentially, the goal is to lightly crush the stem so that it is bent (or even broken), but not snapped. A finger placed behind the stem will brace it and give you a better sense of when the stem is in danger of being pushed too far.

3. With your opposite hand, pull the stem gently over your index finger until it bends sufficiently. It should make an audible cracking noise.

4. Stems may also be pinched to crack them.

5. After super cropping, stems will require one to three days to heal. Small scars on the stem epidermis are normal.

6. Train multiple stems into opposing directions so that they will have maximum light exposure.

7. Stems may need to be super cropped more than once to be trained sufficiently.

8. If a stem is inadvertently snapped, stake it together as close as possible and as quickly as possible. Generally, stems can be saved!

9. The goal is to cause minor trauma in the stems so that they grow larger and stronger, and sideways. The former creates bigger, healthier plants. The latter bows stems out to maximize light exposure. Both result in better yields, which can be as much as 50% higher.

plants in a vegetative state for approximately two weeks after topping. This gives them time to regenerate sufficiently, and to grow new stems and the multiple calyxes that will be the loci for eventual bud growth.

Some gardeners make the distinction between topping and fimming. The difference is a subtle one. Fimming involves a more precise cut, angled into the new growth at the stem top. By cutting on an angle, the theory is that the multiplication of stems/cola associated with topping will be maximized. In my experience, I haven't noticed much of a difference between a top and a fim. That said, it is something you may want to experiment with down the line. I certainly continue to. For now however, I encourage you to top your plants at least once. For the sake of comparison however, on your first grow, leave at least one plant un-topped. This will help you to compare yields at harvest. In my experience, topping boosts yields to as much as double what they were.

Step-by-Step: Super Cropping

1. Pre-super crop: standing tall and straight.

2. Choose places that are between calyxes.

3. A small pinch can break the stem without snapping the top off.

4. Twisting the stem slowly between fingers is also an effective strategy.

5. Bending with slowly increasing pressure also works. Use a finger behind the stem to guard against using too much force.

6. The main stem has now been broken without snapping and stays in this new position.

7. Done: the top of this plant has been bent to 90 degrees, though it will rebound somewhat in coming days.

8. A profile of a super cropped plant, bowed but not broken!

Sun	Mon	Tue	Wed	Thurs	Fri	Sat
	2	3	4	5		7
8	9	10	11	12	13	14
15	16		18	19	20	21
	23	24	25		27	28
29	30					

Month one: Plants move from cloning and germination, almost to the end of vegetative growth. The majority of your work will be here, but appropriate care now will be rewarded down the line.

Day 30

Today, I've raised the lights off the chains and fully onto the hooks. The plants are quite tall now. Otherwise, my lone action is to snip a single necrotic leaf off one of the Kush plants. Sometimes, "doing nothing" is the work: just checking in on the plants and letting them develop. A gardener too keen to intervene can be potentially as harmful as a hovering parent. The plants will actually do most of the heavy lifting themselves.

In the veg room, the seven developing plants needed to be dropped away from the lights again today so more boards were removed. They were also dry and received two liters of water split between the seven plants. Before watering, I noted that the mossy green formations had disappeared as a result of scraping and more judicious watering.

My other job today was an all-round "styling" for the Mother Kush. This meant not only culling dead leaves, but trimming the plant to shape the sides and top into a more managed look. I also cut off a number of low branches that were too small and sparsely covered with leaves to

Cannabis is a resilient plant and can afford to have fan leaves trimmed when compromised. Though opinions on this subject differ, I often remove necrotic leaves early so that plants can devote their full resources to healthy areas.

be viable clones. Unless a branch is able to develop to this point, it is better to prune the plant so that it can divert resources to stems that are in fact viable. Note from the pictures today the sheer amount of material I have taken off the plant. It will recover this in time.

Day 31

Each of the Kush plants was watered one liter today. Note that the bud formations are thickening up nicely. They are looking fat; this is excellent development for this stage in their life cycles. The eventual crop projection is looking good.

What a difference a trim can make! The Mother looks great. Otherwise, only the larger of the vegging plants need water. The smaller ones still have wet soil so, learning from last week's moss development, I back off my watering. The size difference between the two groups of

Pre- and post-trim: note how much more space is created for both new growth and light penetration into the center of this plant.

adolescent plants is now observable not just in height and number of leaves but also in the disparity in stem thickness. Observing stems is a key way of determining maturity.

Day 32

The Kushes are really starting to mature, and the evidence is on the leaves. Today, I can for the first time observe the formation of crystals on the leaves. These crystals (which at times will look sparkly or dusty depending on both strain and relative maturity) contain the same cannabinoids, such as THC and CBD, as the crystals found on the bud itself. This is the good stuff; the point of the whole endeavor. It is a happy development. Though these still have nearly a month to go, they are entering the final phase of their development.

I feed both on the Aggressive Bloom cycle and spin them to equalize the light distribution. I also need to move Thin Kush as far right as possible. In the next day or two, I will have to raise the lights close to their highest position.

In the veg room I also feed today, splitting two liters of Aggressive Growth amongst the seven plants. This is the highest nutrient dose prior to transferring the plants to the bud room. This is the final push of vegetative growth. They will be moved to the bud room in the next week or so.

To facilitate that move, I top all these plants today. Since the larger ones are pushing nine inches tall and the smallest are almost seven inches, these are ready to be topped. This reduces their height on average to a little more than six inches, a little less in a few cases. At this stage in vegetative growth, they should be delayed for two or three days by the topping, then explode into new, larger growth. The result is a more bush-like shape for each plant; they range from almost ten to greater than thirteen inches wide. A cannabis bush is preferable to a long, thin plant for several reasons. A bushy plant will necessarily have a greater number of calyxes

Happy maturity: white crystalized resin now coats the sugar leaves of this Master Kush. Small sugar leaves can be dried and cured with bud. Larger fans with resin can be dried and saved for use in making tinctures and teas.

A successfully topped Tangerine Dream. Several new stems grow where there was previously just one.

You need to keep a close eye out for subtle changes: these fan leaves have some spotting that could easily be missed, and can be an early red flag for emerging problems.

that will translate into greater production of bud for harvest. Also, though the topped stems will be smaller on average than an un-topped terminal cola, which can be huge relative to the rest of the plant, the greater over-all number of stems will increase yields. Finally, the shorter and wider shape of the plant leads to a more uniform stem length. This allows for the light to hit stems more evenly, and to better penetrate the leaf canopy toward the bud formations found on the lowest stems. On un-topped plants, these will in some cases barely develop because they are so far away from the fluorescent T5s.

The only plant that I have decided not to top is the runt Kush, though this is hardly an accurate description any more. It is just as tall as its sisters, post-topping. It is however somewhat unbalanced in its development, quite thick on one side and thin on the other. I could "train" a branch down toward the lighter side with stakes and twist ties, but I opt to leave it be for now.

The differences between the strains are highly evident now. The smaller shape of the indica-dominant leaves on the Master Kush and Pandora are quite different from the longer, slender foliage on the Tangerine Dream plants. The latter also grow much more densely, almost ball-like compared to the Kush. Given the cumulative diameter of these plants, I am starting to become a victim of my own success: I'm running out of space in this room. This is actually a happy place to be as it means a healthy crop of plants. It also isn't a problem in the short term, such as this case where I will be moving at least half of them out into the other room shortly.

I feed the Kush Mother too and notice that it looks pretty wimpy as a result of all the grooming. I need to do this progressively, however, as I want to have enough space in the veg room to maintain not just one Mother, but two. The healthiest of the Tangerine Dreams will, once sexed as female, rejoin the Kush Mother here to serve as a secondary host for clone production. Given that I also require sufficient room to cultivate new clones or plants from seed on an ongoing basis, I really want to keep the Mothers at a manageable size. In retrospect, I would have preferred to limit the growth of the Kush Mother to roughly a foot rather than over two feet tall as it currently stands. This would have avoided the need for such an elaborate setup of shelves and boards in this room for clones and vegging plants which are all well under a foot tall for most of their stay. Shorter Mothers mean lower lights which means less room needed and less hassling with moving plants up and down to meet high lights. Good things come in small(er) packages.

I may, in coming weeks, decide to grow a new Kush Mother; one that I will top out at twelve inches. At that point, I will retire this plant. It is too tall to bring to bud in my current grow situation (it would bypass the lights and hit the ceiling upon experiencing its growth spurt). This is something you can avoid: keep your Mother just large enough to produce viable clones, no larger.

Day 33

I suspect a final growth spurt may be in the offing for the two Master Kush plants. Both were thirsty overnight so I give each plant one liter of water. Even better is the fact that the crystallization has moved into

Be patient with topped plants before moving to flower. They will need time for new stems to grow. Moving them over too soon doesn't allow new locations for bud formations to be fully formed. Haste can make waste, at least in terms of the potential for overall yield at harvest.

the mid-section of each plant. Bud strings, lines of uninterrupted bud, are also present in the lowest stems now. The plants seem hungry so I will feed again in the next day or two since they aren't burnt at all. This is shaping up to be a good harvest.

Post-topping, everything looks good. The cut stem tops have dried nicely and new leaves are clearly taking off. I should be able to trace divergent stem growth over next week, at which time the plants should be ready to move over to the bud room. Based on current growth rates, it looks like the second Tangerine and final Kush should be ready for topping tomorrow. The third and final Tangerine is still on the small side, and is falling behind its sisters to the point at which I am a bit concerned. I'll keep a closer eye on this one over the coming days.

The challenge here is, again, to be patient. I'm getting antsy to move these over to the bud room, particularly the new strains. However, they'll be better served down the line if I wait until they are more fully mature before moving them over (as will I in terms of bud produced).

Vertical growth is nearly done and the explosion of bud growth is set to begin.

Marijuana is at its hungriest at this stage of development: be sure to water and feed frequently to avoid stunting growth.

Day 34

I sped up the feed again today, splitting three liters of Aggressive Bloom between the two plants. Though some people might worry a bit about the idea of pouring chemicals into plants meant for human consumption, it is possible to reduce health impacts by vaporizing, something I would strongly recommend if you are anything more than a casual marijuana consumer. In terms of the nutrients themselves, I'm not concerned: part of my routine prior to harvest is to flush the soil and plants well. This can be accomplished by several days or a week of more intense watering. Better, both in terms of overall effectiveness and to accomplish the same task without waterlogged pots (which leads to more saturated plants and thus a more protracted drying time, post-harvest) is to use a dedicated "flush" agent. This definitely improves the taste of the finished bud. My initial harvests, which I neglected to flush, had a detectable smell and taste that was vaguely chemical-like.

Flushed plants are tastier and no doubt healthier for consumption.

A sure sign that this cannabis plant is ready for transplantation into a larger pot is the roots emerging from the drain holes.

Cannabis plants that are produced in your own daily grow are also the safest in the sense that you control the product, and so know exactly what went into it. Also, there really is a sense of satisfaction in enjoying bud that is a product of your own efforts. It is a proud and gratifying moment – and, after very few crops, a much, much less expensive one. Even a handful of modest harvests will more than offset your initial investment in setting up your daily grow. Over time, you will be able to count the hundreds and thousands of dollars staying in your pocket rather than filling someone else's. There's a good taste to that, too.

On the veg side, I topped the final two Tangerine Dreams. The sole, non-topped plant is the smallish Tangerine. I also checked the holes at the bottom of one of the Kush pots and saw a root sticking out. These are ready to be transplanted to the three-gallon pots. This is a job for the next couple days. I split two and a half liters of water between the seven plants and close up for the night. One little note of concern: I've noticed a few small insects flying around in there the last few days. At first I had thought that this was a coincidence. Now, due to the consistency of their presence, I'm thinking maybe they are signs of the (dreaded) infestation. I'll have to keep an eye on this. If the amount of bugs increases quickly or drastically, it will call for immediate action.

Day 35

Post-feed, the two Kush plants in flower look great. Initially I can't find any evidence of leaf burn. I do eventually ferret out a single singed leaf tip. Not bad: I've brought the plants just up to the edge of their nutrient load. This is a benefit of experimentation and keen observation. They also appear to have maxed out in terms of vertical growth. From here on, at least three and probably four or slightly more weeks from now, they will strictly be ripening.

Tonight it is time to transplant the nearly mature plants in the veg room. Now I run into a roadblock: I've neglected to buy enough soil in advance. I don't have enough to fill seven three-gallon pots tonight. Nuts! Had I planned better, this would have been easy to avoid. Now, the only option is to transplant half and leave the remainder for the next day. This isn't the end of the world, and since this is a time consuming job, I don't mind splitting it up. In addition, the smaller plants aren't in as urgent a need to be transplanted. Potting soil typically comes in 30-liter bags. These will be sufficient for your first grows. However, as you

Vegetative growth really takes off once plants are moved to larger pots. Smaller ones may initially have to be raised and lights adjusted of course.

Step-by-step: Transplanting to Flowering Pots

1. Line the bottom of a new, larger pot with paper.

2. Dig a hole in the pre-moistened soil in the large pot.

3. Make sure the new container is larger than the old one!

4. Gently tap the bottom of the small container to free the plant.

progress, you may wish to buy a larger, more expensive bulk quantity of soil, provided you have enough room in your garden's work area. The bags I now purchase come compressed, and they are almost too heavy for one person to carry unassisted. A bulk purchase is definitely less hassle than having to run errands for soil every couple months. It also reduces a security risk, whereby the prying eyes of neighbors might wonder about bag after bag of potting soil going into your residence. That said, a bulk block of compressed soil is even more conspicuous: a dead giveaway for a home grow operation. I leave mine in the trunk of my car until after dark and then bring it inside to minimize any curious questions.

5. *Hold the soil, not the plant, when removing from the pot.*

6. *Try not to damage the roots when removing the paper from the base.*

7. *Carefully press the plant into the hole in the new container.*

8. *Pat the soil even and trim lower leaves. Now it's ready to thrive!*

Repotted, these plants are now too tall to require any boards to bring them closer to the lights. They will be ready to move this week for sure. Though I watered the soil tonight (remember: space out and minimize your stressors), I would prefer to get in the first Transition feed for this group prior to the move.

I'm feeling pretty satisfied. Though I'm only about a third of the way through the group, time-wise, I feel like I'm halfway through. Barring unforeseen problems, once the plants are transferred over to the 12/12 cycle of the bud room, the majority of work will be over and I can cruise through to the second harvest. Vegging the plants is without a doubt the far more labor intensive phase of growth. But the work looks like it will pay off nicely. Once this is over, the only real labor-intensive job will be sexing the plants grown from seed. This is the major plus for cloning your own plants: once you've successfully sexed and cultivated a Mother plant, this time-sensitive and potentially stressful job can be eliminated.

There is no change on the bug front. They are very small, non-biting and don't make any noise. They are easy enough to kill but there seem to be too many to kill like one would house flies. Hmmmm…

Day 36

In the bud room, I move the left side back onto the chain, now on the upper hook. The right moves up as well and will be on the upper chain imminently as well. The top colas, noticeably thickened, were danger-ously close to a burn tonight. Evidently the vertical progress of these plants isn't quite done.

In the veg room, I've been forced by space limitations to bring out my best Jenga skills. After finishing the re-potting that I started last night on the three smaller plants, I now have to move to additional pans since only two three-gallon pots fit in each pan. Thus, I have no choice but to jerry-rig a structure to accommodate all the plants while not sac-rificing too much light exposure. This pins the Kush Mother somewhat, which is definitely not ideal and would actually be harmful long term. But this is a strictly short-term solution. A good number of these plants will move over in the next few days.

This raises a larger planning issue. On this grow, I currently have a sig-nificant imbalance in terms of the plants split between the two grow rooms: two in the bud room and eight in the veg. What has happened today is the result of this imbalance, and it is something I am likely to come up against on the other side shortly. There could be as many as seven or eight plants in a space that is ideal for no more than four plants, five at most. Each additional plant in the bud room will reduce the light exposure each plant enjoys. This, in turn, will lower the yield per plant. Following this grow, I intend to transition to a more balanced garden: Master Kush and Tangerine Dream Mothers at home in the veg room, with four plants (two of each) vegging at any time. This will leave a space for four budding

An imperfect but temporary solution: boards have been used to raise this smaller vegging plant closer to lights. Those on the plastic shelf to the right are much more stable.

A different solution to a related problem on the bud side: these stems are now supported with stakes and twist ties. As plants grow more heavy with bud, these are essential tools to maintain proximity to lights and even to stop plants from toppling over under their own weight.

plants in the other room. Not only will this be more manageable, it will also maximize light exposure during budding, grant additional time for bud-enhancement interventions while vegging, and will allow for a more balanced schedule of four plants coming to harvest every six weeks, two of each strain for a balanced variety. I've chosen complementary strains that provide a contrast of "day" and "night" pot; do your research in terms of what works best for you! For now, this grow will demonstrate how to deal with a less-than-ideally-balanced grow schedule.

Back to the events of the day: only yesterday I noted the benefits of the less-labor intensive budding stage, save for unforeseen emergencies. As I work tonight, that is exactly what presents itself: while working, I manage to kick over my camera tripod onto the budding Kush. The camera setup is strictly a product of my daily grow book project. It is something you won't likely have to contend with unless you're an amateur photographer as well as novice green thumb. However, a tripod-slam could easily be a spilt beer or dropped light.

I've inadvertently broken two stems on one of the Kush, albeit only minor breaks. Without a fix, these stems would be, best case, further away from the lights than ideal and, worst case, broken to the point of death. Were that to happen, the buds would be too far away from harvest to be salvageable. However, the breaks are minor. With stakes and twist ties, both of which I keep on hand at all times, I am able to correct this unfortunate development. In the end, the affected stems are, if anything, closer to and more directly exposed to the lights. I will keep a close eye on them to ensure that they aren't fundamentally compromised, but I think I've righted the situation.

Day 37

Surveying the results of yesterday's injury-inducing klutziness, the Kush is no worse for wear. The stakes appear to have done their job. Important note here: stakes and ties are the best way to deal with stems broken or

A beginner's mistake: these bamboo stakes are less than ideal as paint can leach into soil. Instead, choose metal stakes from your local garden center.

Planning is everything: avoid exceeding your garden's space capacity or else risk depriving plants of sufficient light. These vegging plants must be turned daily to allow all parts to gain access to light as they are spilling out the sides of this bank of T5s.

bent for any reason, or to move lower stems closer to the lights. They are a valuable resource; never be without them.

I water the Kush and move on to the veg room. The plants are now large enough that I need to spin them daily, not so much to avoid leaning as to ensure that all plants get sufficient light; all but the runty Tangerine are so large that I cannot get them completely under the bank of lights. My plan now is to move the plants over in stages: the three largest in the next couple of days, to be followed by the remaining four in one or even two moves. Given that the small, still un-topped Tangerine is so far behind, this is a must.

I've also spied what I think will be the Tangerine Mother, provided it is indeed female. I'm only a couple of weeks now from figuring this out. I feed Transition to the lot, save for the Mother, which gets its regular (non-bud) nutes. All in all, it has been a long couple of nights working in the garden. Though I had intended to make some measurements tonight, I'm bushed. It's okay to admit defeat. I'll return to this tomorrow.

Ideally, cannabis in your garden should be shaped to form small bushes with multiple stems. This is ideal, not only for creating more locations for bud development, but also for maximizing use of space in cramped conditions.

Day 38

The budding Kushes continue to develop more crystallization. They do, however, appear to be done gaining height, with Thin Kush measuring 25 inches tall, Thick measuring 22, and both just about 22 inches wide, give or take. If so, this will be a bit shorter than my last few summer grows. They have not pushed the lights to their maximum extent. These plants were, however, topped multiple times, creating a much more bush-like form than is typical of the tall, thin Master Kush. I'll double-check the measurements next week to confirm that growth is done. It would be ideal if it were, since it would allow me to focus on the significant growth/movement and sexing of the plants that are about to join these two. I water the two a liter each and am done for the night.

The four largest of the seven vegging plants, which I've decided will be the first to move over to the bud room, get two liters of water, as does the Kush Mother. Speaking of the elder stateswoman of this garden, it's been a bit neglected in terms of grooming of late, not to mention pinched for space. It is definitely due for some serious TLC once the move is done.

All having been topped, the plants have reached mature height. The Pandora is 10 inches tall and the three Kush are just under, just over and just on 10 inches respectively. Each spans more than a foot wide. The Tangerine Dreams are each a couple of inches shorter but two or more wider than their Master Kush counterparts. The outlier is the small Tang that is less than seven high and 10 wide. We are ready for moving day.

Day 39

Moving Day! The three Kushes and the Pandora are moved over to the bud room. This requires shimmying the two mature Kushes to the furthest extent possible to the right, higher side. I can just about fit them all in. Before all is said and done, I will almost certainly have to stake the plants, less to improve proximity to the lights and more to stop them from impinging on one another's space. The only other option involves expense, though it could be worthwhile: buying a second light

What a difference a month makes! Note the differences in size and shape between more mature plants that are budding and new arrivals.

A much happier plant now that, with overcrowding addressed, it has better access to the lights.

This is ideal and evidence of why close proximity to the lights is essential: this Tangerine Dream shows no stretching as evidenced by multiple calyxes forming in close proximity to one another.

for this room. There is enough room for a half-sized (two-foot) light. I'll keep an eye on the plants and decide as the grow develops. It's not a terrible idea. Given the compact space, I (and you) may as well maximize the useable light. I'll need to figure this out fairly soon, chiefly because I want to get at least a couple of the Tangerines in here for sexing purposes. There's no point in continuing to bake one or more of them along in vegetative state, only to find that I've burnt a month or more of grow space, time, and effort on a male that must be destroyed.

In the veg room, things are much more manageable now. The Kush Mother almost audibly sighs with relief. It is no worse for wear having come through the pinned quarters of the last week. I give it a major cull, removing a handful of yellowed leaves, cutting back the sides and topping the canopy. I also dismantle the tower of wood that housed the plants.

The Tangerines are also able to spread out as well. After watering them moderately, I note that the stems are thickening. Though a few weeks behind the Kush, they are maturing. As noted earlier, they are shorter and denser than the Kush. Given that this is my first grow with this strain, I'm guessing a bit regarding when they will be sufficiently mature to transition to budding. I'll research this over the next few days to see if I can better determine this. The final act on this side takes place today – topping the final Tangerine. I think it was wise to wait.

Day 40

Now that I've created more space in the veg room, I can see more clearly that the bugs are indeed a problem: we've got an infestation on our hands. Based on what I've observed and have researched online, I am fairly certain that these are fungus gnats. Damn. These aren't the most serious type of infestation – spider mites, for instance, can total a small garden in wicked time – but this is still a pain in the ass. After some research online, I have learned that fungus gnats are more of a nuisance than a clear and present danger. They are small and kick up when I water or disturb the pots because they nest near the surface of the soil. They are at least potentially dangerous, however, since they will feed on roots. Provided the infestation is kept in check, this isn't supposed to pose a major threat to mature plants, and mine all look just fine. But, for younger plants, these pests can pose a more significant threat. I'm wondering now about the smallest Tangerine. Hopefully its growth hasn't been impacted, though this now seems likely. Fungus gnats appear in conditions with, as their name states, fungus. Generally, they are a problem associated with overwatering and cooler temperatures. I'm afraid, given that my poorly insulated grow rooms have cooled somewhat as winter has approached, and that I did overwater at times over the past month as evaporation slowed with dropping temps. My garden meets both criteria.

That I've avoided infestation of any kind until now is a mixture of luck and diligence: cleaning up after myself on a regular basis and taking good care of the plants. Nothing to be ashamed of here – you show what you're worth as a gardener on the hard days, not the easy ones! Still, I'm curious about the source of the infestation. I'll do some more research online to try to locate potential culprits. I'll also pick the brain

Step-by-Step: Pest Control

1. Contact sticky strips are a good way to avoid insecticides. Don't spray your cannabis with anything you don't want to ingest.

2. Peel back paper and bend pads into plastic stakes.

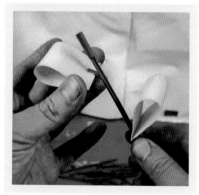

3. Use care when placing insect traps. They will stick to anything they touch and can cause damage to fragile plants.

It is vital that sticky traps are kept away from leaves. Even a simple brush up against a fan leaf will destroy it.

of the resident expert at my local hydroponics/grow store. He may have some insights here. It is closed for the night, but I'll drop in tomorrow in the hopes that there is an inexpensive and low-effort solution.

A quick word about making use of people working at a "local." Now, you may not be lucky enough to live close to a hydroponics or cannabis shop, but if you live in a major city, you almost certainly have one or both not too far away. In my experience, the good people who work in such stores are often passionate about marijuana and growing, not necessarily in that order. Good advice: take your time when shopping. Talk to those who are more expert or experienced than you. Ask lots of questions. Don't be afraid to sound dumb or inexperienced – I've found over the past year that my guy loves to answer questions and particularly to problem solve. Moreover, they are often less likely to push a hard sell than a website hawking one product or another; they tend to under-promise and over-deliver in my experience. In fact, the staff at my local have, over the many months I've dropped in, discouraged me from buying products that aren't strictly necessary; for instance, where

By the fifth week in flowering under a 12/12 light cycle, the bud formations on these Master Kush expand rapidly. So does their smell – take appropriate precautions.

a natural home-remedy might suffice or an expensive gadget has been beyond the scope of my needs. You might even ask if they offer a discount for medical grows. I mentioned licenses in passing and the staff at my local explained that they offer a small discount for clients with medicinal licenses.

In the meantime, since the local is closed for the night, I buzz out for a temporary solution to my gnat problem. The hardware store sells sticky tape traps for gnats. I buy a pack of these. There are a variety of chemical insecticides, but I steer clear of these; remember that anything you spray on or near your plants should be used with caution. My rule is this: if I'd have to think too hard about spraying something near food I'm going to eat, then that is a product that I'm not likely to use in my garden, either. Discretion, being the better part of valor, rules the day. I'll hold the line at the sticky traps and see what I can get from the pros tomorrow.

While already at the hardware store tonight, however, I see an opportunity to save time now that I'm here: I purchase more hooks and chains for the lights I plan to pick up at the local. I also snag another pack of easy-to-assemble plastic shelves to make life easier in terms of stacking plants of various sizes closer to the lights. I return home and set up the traps; at least one per plant and two for the larger ones. Be very careful when setting these up: I was very cautious, and yet I still caught the tip of one leaf and almost a half of a second on the traps – one leaf actually ripped right off the plant. Go slowly! The cure can be worse than the disease if you end up tearing your plants up with bug traps.

Given all the extra work tonight, not to mention a trip to the hardware store, I am thankful that I don't have much other work to do in the garden. None of the plants need water and I just spin them to equalize the light exposure for each.

I'm a bit more concerned about the smallest Tangerine Dream now. Its leaves are slightly browned and the plant looks droopy overall. Still, it has emerging evidence of new leaf growth beginning, so hopefully it will work itself out. The other two Tangerines in the veg room look just fine.

In the bud room, the first noticeable browning is occurring on the tops of multiple buds now. I was worried that these might have been burns from pushing the cola too close to the lights. However, the browning bud includes at least one that could not possibly have strayed too close to the lights, as it is far lower than the larger stems. Maturity is here and the budding/heavy bloom will now begin in earnest. The smell is going to kick up shortly as the harvest approaches. For this reason, I also purchased a few cheap air fresheners tonight while at the hardware store. The smell normally isn't too bad with the Master Kush – other strains like Skunk can be much more potent. However, we are a couple of weeks from Christmas day, and I'm up to host family and friends for Christmas dinner this year. While I'm confident the vent and carbon filters will do their job, and that the cooking bird will cover any lingering scent of my daily grow, I'd rather not have my mother-in-law asking any pointed questions over dinner. Better safe than sorry: buy the air fresheners or incense. I check back in my journal and, working backwards, can time out that these Kush will likely be ready for harvest within a day or two of Christmas. Talk about a fantastic present – and this Christmas, I'm Santa!

Day 41

Tonight is another long night. It takes me more than two hours to complete all my tasks, but this day is an educational and ultimately rewarding one. After visiting my local, I return with the new, small bank of lights for the bud room that I had forecast I would need to maximize use of my space. I find two single, two-foot T5 fluorescents that fit perfectly. What's annoying is that I have to basically disassemble the existing set up of shelves and lights in this room to add the new lights. Once out, I drill holes and install new hooks from which to hang the lights. After adding the chain and linking the two singles to one another to make them more secure (the lights are built to do this), I plug them in to the appropriately timed power bar. Then the room gets put back together and I now have sufficient space to add two of the three Tangerine Dream plants to the three Kush and Pandora plants that just moved over, plus the two older Kushes that are approaching harvest. That brings the total to eight in this room, so the room is still quite full right now and is sure to become downright tight as these newly transferred plants hit their growth spurts a few weeks from now. With any luck, the two mature Kush will move out for harvesting before things get too cramped. When I have more time (and energy) tomorrow, I will stake the most mature Kush to maximize space. This is also necessary because the bud on one cola in particular has thickened to the point that it is

It may be of lower wattage, but a small, single T5 allows a smart grower to maximize their use of space.

The rusting on the fan leaves of this young Tangerine Dream plant is proof that all is not well. Rather than risk the possibility of it spreading, affected leaves are trimmed away from healthy growth.

slumped over on its stem due to its growing weight. This isn't bad news!

The bud room is now sorted out and I can now return to the primary challenge of the last days: the gnat infestation. The staff at my local have suggested that, since my infestation is as yet not too serious, the best initial treatment in terms of being non-invasive is to use Mosquito Dunk. The dunk is a product of natural bacteria that are activated in water. As the name suggests, they are meant to reduce spawning of mosquitos in standing water found in many residential yards. They can, I'm assured, also be used in this situation since the dunk bacteria should attack the gnats and won't impact the plants whatsoever. Well, not so much the gnats themselves, but the gnat larvae that exist in the soil. I'm a bit encouraged that, now that I know to look for them, I don't see any clear evidence of these when I agitate the soil tonight. I hope that means I'm acting quickly enough. One sign that I might be is that the sticky traps have nabbed fewer than half a dozen gnats.

Because the plants need to be treated with the dunk water, I put off the feeding that I had intended for tonight until tomorrow at least. My

Step-by-step: Installing T5 Fluorescent Lights

1. Hooks and chains are a must in order to easily raise and lower lights.

2. It's a good idea to purchase additional replacement bulbs for when old ones burn out.

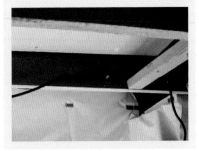

3. Plastic shelves are easy to clean and their height can be adjusted according to your needs. It is often easier to adjust from below by raising plants than by dealing with lights above.

4. Secure all power cords and wires to ensure that they will not fall in water or cause a trip hazard.

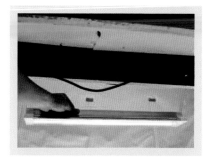

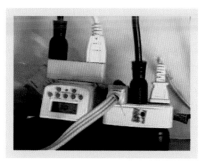

5. Check that the setup will work before placing a plant under bulbs. A dropped light can break a plant stem easily.

6. Ensure that timers are set and power bars are safely out of your work area.

7. Test lights before installing to ensure they are in working order.

8. Many T5 systems allow lights to be linked together to avoid multiple power cords.

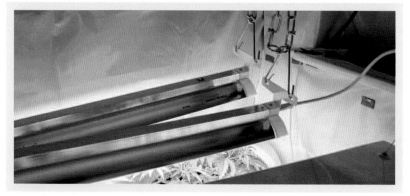

9. Single T5 bulbs are even easier to adjust and are a great way to maximize unused space.

only other job for tonight is to wield the knife: Mother Kush is desperately in need of a trim along its canopy, which is now brushing the T5s. I also engage in some fairly significant surgery to the small Tangerine.

I cut off five fan leaves: half the mature ones. These were looking rugged – spotty, dry, rusty, and browning. I hope this is a case of one big step back to save the plant. Keep in mind that the one Kush clone looked dodgy for a while and now it is going gangbusters in the bud room. In any case, I am flush out of space in the bud room, so the very earliest this final Tangerine can move over is when the two Kushes are harvested in a couple of weeks. I'll use the intervening time to hopefully nurse it back to health. If I'm lucky and it gets better quickly, I'll simply top the plant multiple times, which will add to overall yield down the road, provided it is a female. Remember that like its two sisters and the Pandora, this plant remains unsexed.

Day 42

There's very little action from the gnats today, with only a few flying around and not many new ones caught on the traps. This could be an early sign of good things. Still, I decide to hold off the feed for another day to dry the soil out.

The Pandora and Kush have begun their growth spurts. They needed to be moved away from the lights. I can now see visible signs of female sex on two of the three Kushes. This was never in doubt since they were cloned from the Kush Mother, but still this is a positive sign of development. More exciting is the discovery that the Pandora is also a female. Given that this was my only seed, this is great news. A male would have meant garbage with no recourse for this strain. Given that this was a freebie seed, this is a bonus. It will be interesting to watch it develop.

Regarding the Tangerine Dream plants, the plan now is to wait until they show sex. This should take about a week to 10 days. With any luck they will both be female. In this case, I will return the stronger, healthier looking plant to the veg room to assume the role of Tangerine Mother. The other can be brought to bud. If I only get one female, I will make it the Mother since, even if the Tangerine on life support in the veg room is female and

These white hairs emerge from the calyxes after roughly a week into the 12/12 light cycle. They are your surest signs that you are dealing with female plants, not males. These can been seen earlier under a pocket microscope, but even the naked eye spots these.

can be returned to health, it has been too compromised to serve as a source for clones. In the best-case scenario, it'll be brought to harvest for whatever amount of bud I can coax out of it. The worst case, which is unlikely because these seeds are feminized and even non-feminized seeds average 50% females, is that both Tangerines in the bud room are male. If this happens, I will have to grow a couple more from seed. This would set me back about six weeks, but wouldn't be the end of the world.

Day 43

All the plants are fed today. As a result of the gnat infestation, I'm a bit shy about over-watering. Still, I balance this against the possibility of nutrient deprivation. Nutes win. Newly moved plants get a Transition feeding while the more mature plants get Aggressive Bloom and Aggressive Growth in the Bud and veg rooms respectively.

Evidence of infestation: fungus gnats on sticky traps.

Careful not to over-water: runoff into the pans is normal, but waterlogged pots invite pests and can compromise roots and stems.

There is still very little gnat action. It seems too soon for the mosquito dunk to have taken effect; it is supposed to take several days for the chalky material I broke up into the treatment water a couple of days back to work properly. No need to complain though, fingers crossed. The other positive development today is the effect of adding the new bank of lights to the bud room. The plants are enjoying much more even access to the light. This was a good call. Provided you can afford the equipment, maximizing the small space for a home grow is one of the best ways to ensure the success of your garden.

The Kush Mother is looking a little ragged. Since the last trim and thin it has been dropping yellow leaves at an accelerated rate. Though Mother plants aren't typically much work, when they're showing any significant amount of distress, you should dedicate extra attention to them. The key decision to make in the case of a fundamentally compromised Mother is salvaging as many viable clones as possible before it is beyond saving. Failure to do this in time can result in losing your

Mother and having to start over from seed.

The Tangerine gets a day off; its soil is still moist so it doesn't need water and it is too small to make a spin necessary. A feed is, for the time being, out of the question. As soon as new growth has taken hold, I will hit it. On that note, the leaf shoots on the main stem seem bigger today – I think they are taking off and I'm now willing to bet this plant will make it. See: it is important not to jump to conclusions. While it's good to be vigilant and act quickly, I thought this plant was a goner for sure a couple of days ago. Now it looks better. So there you go: it ain't called "weed" for nothing!

Day 44

Today I'm able to further confirm the sexing from earlier this week. The third Kush is showing its sex, the Pandora is more pronounced in its production of white pistils and none of the plants demonstrate any aspect of hermaphroditism. The Tangerines are still not showing sex and have yet to grow much since the move, but they look healthy. Each has

These flowering cannabis plants are organized on three different levels to accommodate plants in different stages of development. A surprising number of plants can be accommodated under a single four foot T5 light set up. The additional lights accommodate the two plants in the back.

Topping has slowed the development of this Tangerine Dream. But the investment in extra time will be worth it down the line when multiple colas develop rather than a single terminal stem.

small shoots on its stems. An important note here: it is easy to mistake new shoots at the calyxes for the "pistil" shape of female sexing. I mistakenly sexed a couple of males as females early on my first grow and thought, "wow, I got really lucky; all females!" This was most definitely not the case. Until there is a pronounced production of white hairs, you can't say for sure whether your babies are female or not. Still, this is evidence of stem development and all-round health, so it is a good sign.

In the veg room the Tangerine's two highest fan leaves continue to look strong. The three remaining lower fan leaves are looking more necrotic but hanging in there. Were there more full growth on this plant, these leaves would have been pinched off already. However, while I don't want to drain the plant's energy on dying leaves – or to spread any problem through the plant (or worse, to others) – I think if I ditch these too early, the plant may give it up. It's better to give them another few days if possible, by which time the new leaf growth should have taken hold.

On the gnat front, the total count on the sticky traps is about a dozen across both rooms. No sign of a single gnat flying today despite watering, moving pots and cultivating the soil (in an attempt to disturb their breeding grounds). This is a very good sign; if this pans out and I got them, I am surprised at the ease. Either I really did move quickly, or got lucky, or both.

Day 45

There's not much to say today because I took my first day off. This is a little reward for me since today unofficially marks the mid-point of this grow, at least for the Kush; I'm beginning to think that the Tangerine Dream may take somewhat longer to fully mature. My close associate, who I trust and have trained to take care of most day-to-day tasks when I go away, tended the garden. This is something to consider before starting your daily grow: determine a person (or two) who can stand in for you if necessary. If you are tied to your garden, unable to go away for a weekend for instance, you will soon resent it and/or ruin a crop through neglect. A trusted co-gardener is a must. Mine is a real green thumb who is interested in learning, so this is a win-win situation.

No elbowroom: account for space restrictions when planning when plants need to be cultivated and moved from veg to bud.

When space is restricted, it is especially important to turn plants regularly to ensure that all parts of the plant get good exposure to the fluorescent lights.

Take regular measurements of your plants to compare development across successive generations, to note the impacts of topping and super cropping and to get a sense of when each strain is ready to move to flowering.

Day 46

An important tip to start today: I would have spilled a quarter bottle of the FloraBlend feed had I not tightened the cap between measuring feeds, which is today's major task. I should have known as it's been a klutzy day all round; I spilled coffee on myself earlier in the car. Always tighten your caps!

For the next week I've decided to spotlight one plant per day to observe the development of each in more detail. Today I am focusing on the Pandora: it has nine (!) separate cola formations. This is great. It should make for a tidy haul at harvest time. It is now more than 13 inches tall and slightly wider than that again. Bud is also beginning to form at the lower calyxes. This is an excellent development for this young plant. The Pandora is definitely maturing more quickly than the Master Kush or Tangerine Dream. The tops of each stem look a bit wilted but growth continues to be robust underneath so this may just be a peculiarity of the strain.

Its leaves are short and compact, indicative of an indica-dominant strain. It's tough to say as this is my first go around with this strain, but I suspect this may be an aspect typical of the development of Pandora.

Day 47

Some minor movement of lights and shelves today to accommodate growing plants but no need to water anything. In the spotlight today is Kush #1. Like the Pandora, this plant is approximately 13 inches tall and wide. It has four main stems, each topped by a well-developed bud, round and shaped like a button. This is typical for this stage in its development. Otherwise, this is a quiet day. Other than an irritating surge in the number of gnats flying around, and a corresponding number caught in the sticky traps, there's not much to do or report.

The fungus gnats are still on the scene. Replace traps regularly to get a sense of whether infestations are getting worse or better.

Day 48

In the spotlight today is Kush #2. Like its sister, this plant is 13 inches tall. It is wider, though, measuring 15 inches across at the widest point. From a bird's eye view, four major and two slightly less pronounced stems are evident. I predict that this plant will produce a slightly larger amount of bud at harvest. On lower branches, development of white pistil hairs continues: they are thickening and growing longer. These should develop into the larger bud formations along each stem as the plant matures. This one looks to be the pick of this particular litter.

The other plants in the bud room are fine. There's no need for watering but I spin all plants to equalize light distribution today. There's still no sign of sex on either Tangerine. They're a bit tardy but should show in the coming week. This isn't a major concern. There is a "sexing window" of about a week, give or take, once sex characteristics begin

Thin (left) and Thick (right) Master Kushes might differ in height, but both are rewarding my efforts with thick bud formations on the terminal colas.

The two remaining necrotic fan leaves are removed from this Tangerine Dream. Despite the delay, it is now taking off with healthy growth.

to manifest themselves. You needn't worry about sexing plants prematurely (and incorrectly), as it is okay to take a few days to identify the sex of each plant correctly and beyond a doubt before removing any males. In the other room, the Mother Kush looks a bit better today, with fewer necrotic leaves.

The lone Tangerine still vegging has lots of new leaf growth and is getting taller. For the first time, it needs to be moved away from the lights. Having responded well to the last feed, it seems likely that it will be well developed and ready for the move when the Kushes are harvested. The three necrotic leaves can now be removed.

Day 49

In the spotlight today is Kush #3. Despite a less full appearance, this plant has recovered fully from the minor trauma it encountered while vegging. It is a foot tall and 14 inches wide. It has four main colas and several smaller ones. It has largely filled out and it is no longer obvious

This Master Kush is viable despite its uneven vegetative growth. Training stems to fill in gaps has created a well-developed plant.

Grown from a sexed clone, this was sure to be a female. Still, it is worth checking even previously sexed plants to ensure that none have gone hermaphrodite in response to stress, as this one might have.

that this plant was unbalanced, with one side full and the other hollowed out. This Kush stands as an example of why, in many cases, you needn't give up on plants that have undergone trauma. As well as the satisfaction of successfully nursing a plant back to health, you will often be rewarded with a healthy and full harvest. The extra time nursing a plant back to health is always going to be worth it when compared to starting a new clone or seed from scratch.

This holds for the lone Tangerine Dream still vegging in my garden. Today, its recovery looks complete and it has returned to normal growth. Soon, it will be ready for topping and eventual transfer to the bud room. Otherwise this is a quiet day: I give Mother Kush some water as I've dried the soil out in an attempt to tamp down the gnats. One more day would have been a problem, however, as I can see the droop in its leaves. I spin the plants for light distribution but not much else. There are still no obvious sex characteristics on the Tangerines in the bud room but they should be showing imminently.

Remember to take a look from up above! The tendency will be to observe plants from the side and neglect the top. A look down at the plant (with lights removed) will give you a sense of how much light can penetrate to lower branches.

This Tangerine Dream has just been moved for flowering. Expect an explosion of vertical growth in the first two to three weeks after moving to 12/12 and move lights accordingly.

These are new leaves, not the more typically white, hair-like pistils that indicate a female: don't confuse the two when sexing plants.

Day 50

In the spotlight today: Tangerine Dream #1. Though, like its sibling, this Tangerine has yet to definitively show its sex, there does appear to be the development of pre-bud formations at the top of each stem. The stems themselves are thick and healthy and, in a development particular to this strain, show an orangey coloring at points in the stem's flesh. They literally look tangerine. The bushy development is significantly more compact overall than the Kush; the major challenge for this variety will be growing the plants in such a way that light is able to penetrate into the dense center of each plant. I may opt to stake or otherwise train the branches if this appears to be a problem. Since this is my first go-around with this strain, I'll wait on this for the time being to have a more accurate base line for their development patterns.

The two maturing Kushes now have a rusty orange coloring even in the lower sections of each plant. Though the changing color of the bud has advanced to most parts of the plants, the overall coverage is significantly less than the 75% color change when I typically harvest. The smell has strengthened though, particularly if the plants themselves are brushed in passing. I try to avoid this though, and you should too, as it disturbs the THC-laden resins on the plant. The Pandora is sprouting white hairs everywhere; this will all develop into bud. Its major growth spurt appears to have begun. I'll have to juggle the lights and/or supports if the other plants don't keep pace. I feed all plants in both rooms today.

Day 51

In the spotlight today is Tangerine #2. It has developed in tandem with Tangerine #1, though the latter has more green tendrils emerging at the calyxes. Though these are both maturing much more slowly than the Kush, I'm hopeful that they will develop into white hairs shortly so that I can sex them. This is now my first task of each gardening session. You will want to sex your plants as early and definitively as possible to avoid contaminating your garden with any male interlopers. After a little further reading into the Tangerine Dream strain today, I am now aware that, as sativas, these cannabis strains typically take a third longer to develop than their indica counterparts. This perhaps explains the delay in displaying sex.

The Kush are nearly mature now. I will likely feed them one more time on the Ripen schedule, which has a reduced nutrient load. Then I will flush them one or more times over the period of a few days. Since these are close to harvest, I'll also start to suss out suitable stems on the Kush Mother to make replacement clones for these two that are about to depart.

Day 52

In the spotlight today is Tangerine #3. Though deeply compromised before, this plant is nearly ten inches tall and almost 15 inches wide. It looks phenomenal – a story of both success and perseverance. I'm glad I didn't give up on it.

I water only Mother Kush today as it is a bit dry but everything else is still moist from yesterday's feed. I'm starting to become a little concerned about the burnt out look of this plant, particularly in the entirety of the area below the uppermost canopy. It continues to shed a larger

Sativas mature more slowly than indicas in every respect. This means that this Tangerine Dream will take longer to show sex characteristics.

than normal number of yellowed, even burnt looking leaves from the lower branches. Still the canopy is lush and healthy looking. This will need to be monitored. On the subject of monitoring, I replace the sticky traps on Mother Kush since they had far more trapped gnats than any of the others. A clean slate will make it easier to judge the extent of continued gnat action.

Day 53

The temperatures outside are plunging now and this has wreaked a bit of havoc in my less-than-well insulated grow rooms. Checking the temperature, it is barely 60°F in the antechamber, away from the warmth of the lights. This is pushing the bottom threshold of what a grow room should be at, and is significantly below the ideal for room temperature. To address this, I've purchased a small space heater and set it up between the two rooms. It will take a bit of trial and error to get the temperature

Step-by-Step: Raising a Plant to the Light

1. Plastic shelving with adjustable legs provides a stable base.

2. Wooden planks allow for more specific adjustments with a tall plant nearby.

3. Advantage: planks can be removed easily as plants grow.

4. Ensure pots are centered on raised platforms to avoid a fall.

5. Close proximity to lights is essential, particularly with lower wattage T5 fluorescents.

6. A cola that is compact and un-stretched: good job!

Before and after: after sexing, the eventual bud sites begin tentative blooming. (left). On the right, the more mature bud is fully formed and recognizable.

right, but consider this as a counterpart to the fan(s) you will likely want for warmer times of year. It is an inexpensive option: the heater itself cost only $20 and I've calculated based on the wattage that it will add less than five dollars a month to my electrical bill, even if it runs 24/7, which it shouldn't need to. To this end, I purchased a unit that has an auto shut-off feature, albeit not one with a digitized readout, so I'll have to play with this a bit. More importantly, and this is a must, I bought a heater that has emergency shut-off in the case of overheating or tipping. This reduces the fire hazard to almost zero. Don't skimp: most new heaters, even the cheap ones, will have these built in. Resist the temptation to re-sort to some old heater you've dug out of storage. It isn't worth burning down your garden and home with it to save a few bucks! The other safety consideration is the danger of spilling water on the heater. Given the setup of my garden, I've placed the heater on a raised section of the floor so that, in the case of a major spill, the heater will not be hit with water. The only thing worse than fire might be electrocution. No thanks.

This was the only job for today, save for a little game of "switcheroo". That is, I took the unprecedented step of moving the Pandora back to the veg room. Why? After doing some reading about the Pandora last night, I just had a hunch that the wilted leaves at the top of the plant were not right somehow. When in doubt, hit the Internet, kids! I found out that since it is an autoflowering strain, the plant's blooming cycle is not photo (light) sensitive. It doesn't need the 12/12 cycle to start blooming, but instead it moves at its own pace, determined by an internal, biological timer if you will. I also learned that, given this, autoflowering strains can remain in the 18/6 light cycle; in fact that is preferred, as less light can stunt their growth.

Autoflowering strains tend to turn over faster in terms of crop (a plus!) but, for obvious "body clock" reasons, you cannot keep an autoflowering strain as a clone mother. Though it is possible to take clones from an autoflowering plant, it's not possible to keep one consistent mother. They are, however, a good solution for a beginner grower who does not have room for dedicated veg and bud rooms. Autoflowering strains allow a gardener to cultivate plants solely in an 18/6 light cycle, or even a continuous 24 hours per day of light, unbroken by darkness. We will see how the plant responds to the longer daily light exposure.

Day 54

Well, it definitely isn't too cold anymore. The room was stifling when I entered this evening, approximately 85°F, no doubt warmer under the lights. I reduced the temperature setting for auto shut-off and decided to recheck the room temperature later tonight and tweak it if necessary. Checking five hours later, the temp had dropped to a more comfortable (perfect, actually) 72°F. Mission accomplished.

Upon closer inspection of the maturing Kushes, a fair estimate is that at best 20% of the bud has changed color. Though these are due to be harvested in about a week, I think they might need an extra week, maybe more. It is possible that the colder temperatures slowed their maturity. The final Tangerine Dream, smaller than the others but still healthy and full now, joined the others in the bud room today. Still lack-

Plumped up and almost ready for harvest: these Master Kush warrant close observation to decide when they have reached the optimum harvest window.

ing any definitive sign of sex by observation, I resorted to use of the hand microscope today to attempt to sex the plants. No luck with Tangerine #1, and #3 has only just moved over so there's no point in even checking. There are, however, clear white pistils developing on Tangerine #2, observable using the microscope. I generally only use the microscope for determining readiness for harvest, to gauge the maturity of the trichomes that are the telltale sign of when to pull the plug and harvest. I find the microscope easy enough for this use: the trichomes are plentiful enough that focusing is easy. This is less true of using the microscope to sex plants. Generally, it's safer to wait until you can sex plants with the naked eye. However, I'm excited to find out how these plants, new to my garden, are developing. The microscope has provided a bit of good news. Still, I proceed like a journalist with sexing: you ideally want, at the very least, repeated confirmations or ideally two independent reports to verify facts – it is easy to get it wrong the first time. So I'm cautiously optimistic that Tangerine #2 is a female, but I'll be able to confirm that in the coming days.

Be patient when sexing new plants. These Dreams are close but it is still too early to tell whether they are male or female.

Day 55

Watering had to be kicked up again tonight, as temperatures are now significantly warmer than they have been. The Pandora has responded well to the move back to the veg room; it was nearly kissing the light and the shelves underneath it had to be moved down. This is good preparation in any case as one of the Tangerines will be rejoining the Kush Mother in the coming week or so, taking its place as the new Tangerine Dream Mother. Having the first confirmed signs of female sex characteristics on Tangerine #2 yesterday, I am now feeling more confident that the others will also be female as they have many of the same characteristics. Finalizing these conclusions is very close now. We are about to move into the final, lowest intensity "third trimester" of the plants' development, and the one with the least amount of work required of the gardener.

These are not evidence of female sex characteristics. Growth at these calyxes grows into new leaves, not evidence of budding.

Day 56

There's no water for any of the plants today. It probably wouldn't hurt to give them some, but I've decided to continue to reduce and limit the water they get in order to stem the tide of gnats. They persist, though at a reduced rate.

Today, Tangerine #2 was moved back to the veg room. It is my choice for Tangerine Mother. Why? Two reasons: first, female sex characteristics have shown, by eye, in all three plants, but this is the only one that I checked and double-confirmed using the microscope. Second, it is the all-round healthiest and heartiest looking of the three. All the previous trauma eliminates Tang #3 and, despite its larger size, Tang #1 isn't as impressive as its sister. Also, I think I will get a nice yield off it, so I'm going to leave it to ripen.

I could wait a few more days before returning it to veg, if only to confirm beyond a shadow of a doubt that it is female. I am confident about its sex, however, and every day it is left in the bud room will lengthen the amount of time needed to return it to the vegetative state. Also, the further along it gets in terms of budding, the greater the stress in returning it to veg; this is a potential "hermie risk" so I'm moving today. Some experts suggest cutting a clone from vegging plants then exposing them to a 12/12 light cycle to confirm female characteristics. This method of moving the entire plants is, however, just as fast if not faster and just as sure. Provided the Mother-to-be isn't left to fully bud,

A successful "top" – two stems replace the original single.

Increased growth is the result. The intervention will mean more bud down the line.

the stress of it should be minimal. I have yet to have a problem proceeding this way.

Measuring today, the three Kushes now average 16 inches in both directions, though Kush #3 is a slightly shorter 13 inches. All three have clear signs of bud development now. The Tangerines are a far more bush-like 11 inches tall and almost 20 wide. Tangerine #3, still catching up, is nine tall and 14 wide. They haven't sprouted into full-on bud yet but the female pistils are present and growing. Given that they took longer to appear, the bud will, logically, take longer than the Kushes as well. The Kushes almost ready for harvest have not changed in dimensions for some time as the plants are done growing and are devoting their resources to the maturing bud. The Pandora is 15 by 15 inches and looking great.

The only disquieting observation today is the continued yellowing of the Kush Mother. I am now leaning towards cloning potential replacements, and soon. This is shaping up to be a holiday project. I will monitor closely and intervene early if necessary.

Dead woman walking? This mother's growth wasn't brought under control in time to make it viable for the grow space. Be sure to trim and train your mothers early.

Day 57

I've decided not to wait. The Kush Mother is running shy of branches that present good candidates for cloning. I'd rather preemptively clone a couple, which I do today, and find that I acted with unnecessary haste. I believe I've determined the problem: this plant, which is now nearly nine months old, is likely suffering from "nutrient lock." That is, because I didn't flush the soil on a regular basis (subsequently, I have a regular monthly schedule for this in place of a regular feed), the accumulation of salts has effectively blocked the absorption of nutes by the plant. In retrospect, common sense dictates that the soil would need to be renewed or in some way refreshed from time to time. With a monthly flush using the prescribed flush solution, this is an avoidable problem – one I will avoid in future grows and that, armed with this foreknowledge, you can avoid in the first place.

After having taken the clones, I take evasive action: a full flush of the plant, and a repotting in new soil. The root ball, which I trim and break up as much as possible, is hard as a rock. The work is tough going but

Almost ready to harvest, these Master Kushes are thick and covered with resin.

When heavy with bud, you may have to stake your plants to keep them close to the lights.

eventually accomplished. With luck, this plant will recover. If not, the clones should cover my ass. I'll also take more clones, if the Mother's health allows me to.

It's a bit of an afterthought after all the work in the veg room tonight, but checking in on the two ripening Kushes, I have their pistils at roughly 40% brown now. Half is the minimum threshold and 70-80% is ideal. We're getting closer to harvest now.

Day 58

Since the day after tomorrow is Christmas Day, I did a bunch of dirty work today so that I can keep tasks minimal during a busy family visit. The soil is still moist in all the pots so watering isn't necessary, but the shelves need more than a tweak. They are rejigged to maintain all plants at a healthy distance from the lights.

Small in stature, but thick with bud: this Pandora thickens up on its own schedule, maturing beside vegging plants under the 18/6 light cycle.

Checking Mother Kush, it seems no worse for wear after yesterday's flush, repotting, and canopy trim. Pandora now has bud forming in continuous lines up each major cola. The bud forming is much whiter than that of the Master Kush; the latter is more yellow and creamy even at the earliest stages. The Pandora is almost white by comparison. Though the plant is nowhere near as tall as the Kushes I've grown to date, it has a healthy number of stems and it appears it will have a good amount of bud development. I depart for the night, readying for holiday plans with the garden as locked down as I can get it.

Day 59

The night before Christmas and all through the house, not a creature was stirring... except for the one in the garden: me. Today I started germinating two Deimos seeds, a different variety of autoflowering strain that I have on hand. Having learned about how to best handle these

Step-by-Step: Germinating Seeds

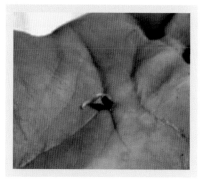

1. Keep seeds warm and moist until they sprout. No soil yet!

2. A sprout, ready for planting.

3. Moisten soil and prepare a shallow hole.

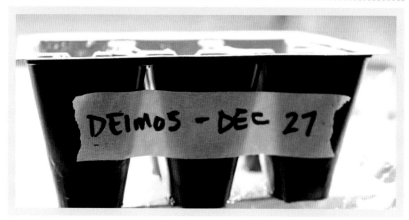

4. Remember to label and watch new seedlings until they grow strong.

This Master Kush is mature and almost ready to move over to budding. Be careful not to overdo the nutes.

from my experience with the Pandora, I've made sure I've got adequate space in the veg room and we're good to go.

The leaves on the Kush Mother, even the uppermost ones that have been the healthiest, are dead: dry and brittle to the point of crumbling in my hand when touched. We will yet see if the intervention to address the soil lock will save or kill the patient. I water the other plants as needed so that I will be able to restrict my gardening to a quick check in only.

The two ripened Kushes are now well over 50% red. They are flushed with the flush solution tonight so that they will be ready for harvest either a day or two after Christmas. The other budding plants all look good. The younger Kushes are now approaching the size of their harvest-ready relatives. Each had a single necrotic leaf as well as slight burns caused by overdoing the nutes. And a real Tangerine moment here: when nipping a leaf off of one of these there is a clearly detectable citrus smell. Weird, but very cool.

Sun	Mon	Tue	Wed	Thurs	Fri	Sat
		31		33	34	
36	37	38	39	40	41	42
43	44	45		47	48	49
50	51	52	53	54	55	56
	58	59	60			

The second month of budding is done, and with it, the Master Kush. The next crop of Tangerine Dream and Pandora are underway. Most of the sweat comes in the first weeks – this is the fun time to watch the results of your efforts.

Day 60

Well, this is the definition of a not-so-merry Christmas: a major emergency in the grow room, with a full house no less. To save time, I had done a quick visual check in the afternoon while the plants were in their dark cycle. The green light allowed me to have a glance at the garden, and everything was fine. After dinner however, a member of my dinner party, who is also my substitute gardener when I need to be away from home, asked for a peek at the garden's progress. What we discovered was a leak from a water pipe that feeds the outside of the house: the hose had been turned off but the line, undrained, had suffered a very minor rupture caused by the ice expanding in it. Normally, this wouldn't be a big deal at all: it appears that, since the water line itself is shut off, it is merely dripping the remnants of the melting line. However, in this case it is a big deal: the water has run down the tube of the exhaust fan, through the fan and carbon filter and formed a small puddle on the floor of the grow room. Ho ho – NO!

Keeping Your Grow Room Clean and Tidy

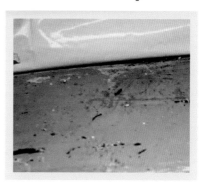

1. *Clean up spills when they occur, not later.*

2. *Dirt and dead leaves can attract pests – deal with it.*

3. *Vacuum up spills.*

4. *Sterilize all areas regularly with vinegar.*

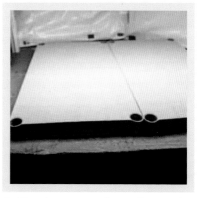

5. *Trays should be wiped down, too.*

6. *Good as new – cleaned up and ready for the next grow.*

Luckily, with a second set of helping hands, we make quick work of this. We proceed methodically:

1. We kill power and unplug appliances. Safety first.

2. We assess the leak source (described above).

3. The fan is unhooked and the carbon filter is drained of the small amount of water that had accumulated in it. Assessing the situation, it doesn't appear that any of the equipment has been damaged. This is unbelievably good fortune (a Christmas miracle?) given that the water ran straight through the fan, past its motor.

4. We remove all plants from the room and disassemble the shelves to allow maximum access to clean up the mess and reassemble the fan and exhaust system.

5. Use the opportunities that present themselves! Given the opportunity to access the whole room, I clean up the small amount of water and vacuum up the room. Given how messed up things are, this is an opportunity to really clean house.

6. The fan is replaced and restarted. Checking its performance, it seems fine.

7. The shelves are reassembled and the plants replaced.

8. We give thanks to Father Christ-Myth that things weren't worse. What a pain in the ass tonight. It could have been far worse though.

With the emergency resolved and the room put back together, I quickly check the other room. Mother Kush continues to dump burnt leaves out of its top center, though there does appear to be some new growth. Mother Tangerine and the Pandora continue to grow, and boards need to be removed from underneath each as they are getting taller. What an exhausting end to the day!

Day 61

Today, a post-script to yesterday's mayhem: with more time and no houseguests, I survey the rooms to ensure that there won't be a repeat of last night. Upon closer inspection, I discover that the exhaust fan is

Set up correctly, after the fact. Check and recheck your set up to avoid costly errors.

Merry Christmas! This Master Kush is ready for harvest.

sucking air into the room from the outside rather than blowing the room's air out through the carbon filter. What a dummy! This isn't a goof from last night. I had installed the fan upside down when setting this room up initially. It was an easy enough mistake to make: the instructions were gobbledygook and I installed the fan atop the carbon filter intuitively, with the writing on the unit's exterior right side up. As it turns out, it actually needs to look upside down. It may seem unbelievable to have missed this for so long, but it is only when I place my hand on the exposed venting tube to outside, expecting to feel air blowing out from the fan and instead having my hand sucking onto the tube opening like a vacuum cleaner would do, that I realize my error. It actually takes a moment to sink in that this is wrong. This comes to light despite the fact that I took my time when setting up the room. The lesson here: double and triple check your set up, and, when you inevitably find errors like this – and there are many more errors that are possible – learn from your mistakes, make the fixes, and move on.

Judging Readiness for Harvest

1. The "Jude" Rule: As my obscure friend advised me when I was starting out: when in doubt, give plants a couple of extra days before harvesting. You have a window – don't be over-anxious!

2. Flush plants before harvest to minimize the chemical taste that can accompany the use of nutrients. Ideally, flush twice in the last week, but at least once, a minimum of two to three days before harvest. Again, it is best to experiment here with the number and duration of flushes prior to harvest.

3. Use a 30x magnifying glass to determine readiness. Trichomes should be mostly cloudy with many turning amber and beginning to shrivel. If trichomes are clear, the bud is unripe.

4. Use the calendar. Make it a habit to label pots with the expected due date from the day that plants have been brought to flower. This typically will be something like sixty days from the day plants are moved into the 12/12 light cycle. Note that most strain reviews make estimates based on use of more powerful lights; using T5 fluorescents may require that plants be given a few additional days or even a week before harvesting according to seed directions.

5. Watch the color of the leaves. Leaf necrosis and loss of chlorophyll (green color turning to yellow on fan leaves), particularly in the bottom third of the plant provides a typical indication of harvest readiness approaching.

6. Look for bud color. By the naked eye the color of the bud is (generally) also an excellent indicator of readiness. Look for 70%+ coloring. This will vary by strain, of course.

7. Note that bud may be ready even though it looks unripe to the naked eye. If the calendar indicates an approaching due date, use the microscope.

8. Know your strain. Follow the instructions. If the information is not provided for you, you can find it online.

9. Keep a grow journal so you have a good, anticipatory sense of when plants will be ready for harvest. Plan ahead! Clear your schedule as harvesting can take 30 to 60 minutes per plant. Multiple plants harvested at the same time can take a full evening.

So many things make sense now: the plunging room temperatures were caused more by the fan sucking cold winter air into the room 24/7 rather than poor insulation. The ineffectiveness of the fan and carbon filter in totally killing the smell of the plants, particularly at harvest, now makes sense. With the fan installed properly, I should be able to dispense with the air fresheners. Not surprisingly, with the fan actually venting and the filter doing its job, the smell in the garden and home beyond the garden is no more. Here is the proverbial silver lining in the cloud (or leak) of the last couple days.

The Kushes are now heavy with bud, so much so that several stems hang down away from the lights. Though I've decided to give them another day or two before harvesting, I don't bother staking these weighed down stems. Were this much earlier in the life cycle of these plants, staking would be a no brainer. For now though, they are fine. Happily, the two Tangerines are now showing the development of bud structures. They are way behind the Kush in developmental terms but are moving along now. It appears that I have 100% females in this grow. This is excellent news, and it's actually a first for me, too.

Day 62

According to the calendar, the Kushes are now three days overdue. The bud is big and seems ready; the smell is there and the crystals are there. The only thing different is that this particular crop is significantly more green and white as opposed to the rusty orange that is typical of this strain. There is a harvest window of about a week, which I'm well within. In fact, you should experiment with harvesting plants of the same strain at different times (say 55 days of bloom, then 58 days, 62 days, 65 days, 68 days, etc). Based on the maturity and/or breakdown of the THC in the ripening process, you will be able to produce bud with subtle but definite differences in terms of finish. I've harvested as early as 55 days, but my average is about 60. I'm curious to let these go to 65 just to see if it improves the quality of the harvest.

I give each plant a little water, which is never a bad idea at this time, to make sure that the plants are fully hydrated when harvested. This

Sativas typically take longer to mature. But these sativa-dominant hybrids look to be worth the wait.

Keep plants moving so that light can penetrate into the centers and hit lower branches. You will be rewarded with more bud sites and better bud.

sounds counter-intuitive: why water plants you are about to dry out? However, it really is better as plants that are too dry at harvest might dry too quickly after it. A slower dry and cure from moistened plants will lead to a better tasting crop.

I also check the trichomes; regardless of the color the bud shows to the naked eye, the trichomes will often show a result that would seem to be inconsistent. For instance, the trichomes might have moved from clear to cloudy to amber, even though the bud hasn't changed color. This turns out to be the case today. The microscope shows trichomes that are mostly amber and starting to wilt. These plants should be harvested straight away.

The younger three Kushes are now as much as 18 inches tall and the same across the main body of each plant. Even the smaller Kush has nearly caught its sisters. The Tangerines are 14 inches tall each, 20 and 14 wide respectively. The Pandora is not quite as tall as the Kushes but is equally wide across. It has responded very well to the return to the 18/6 light cycle. The Tangerine Mother, now pushing 11 inches tall, must be topped for the first time. I am leaning now towards retiring the Kush Mother and replacing it with one of the clones. It not only seems too far gone to act as a Mother, but also a newly grown Mother Kush will allow me to ditch the current monster that I let grow to in excess of two feet tall. The replacement will, like the Tangerine Mother, be kept at a consistent height of one foot tall.

Day 63

Today is harvest day for the two Kushes that pre-dated the start of this grow diary. One at a time, the plants are clipped at their base and cut along the main stem on diagonals so that each stem that will hang on the drying line as if it had a hook. Large fan leaves are removed by gently pulling them off. Smaller leaves are clipped with the scissors. Finally, each stem is manicured: as much excess leaf as possible is removed from amongst the bud on each stem. I tend to err on the side of caution, leaving a bit more leaf on rather than potentially cutting off valuable bud. In fact, when small leaves are heavily dusted with crystallization, I tend to

Despite the much smaller size, this Pandora makes up for it with multiple colas with plentiful bud development.

leave those be as they are laden with THC. I also try not to jostle the crop too much to minimize disruption of said crystals. Once the stems are hung in the drying chamber, a dark closet with string lines is ready for hanging, I turn on the small fan in the room to promote air circulation. They will be left for several days now until they're ready to be clipped at the stems and bottled in Mason jars for further curing.

I won't disturb the drying bud for the next several days. I generally start checking readiness for bottling after three nights of drying. Some grow guides discuss drying times of up to two weeks. This will depend very much on the conditions of your grow situation, however. In my experience, the bud I've harvested is ready to go after a few days, far short of a week. This is because the environment is very dry. Even in the more humid summer months, a dehumidifier operating in close proximity draws the moisture out of the bud fairly quickly. The bottom line is that the bud is ready to be jarred and cured when the stems are brittle and splinter slightly when bent. Stems that are too green and bend fully are not dry enough, while stems that break completely when bent are over-dried. It isn't rocket science. Just experiment, make observations, and take notes on your first and subsequent harvests, being sure to notice environmental conditions and key changes as well as the plants themselves. You will refine your practice quickly.

Having the harvest out of the way, today's other big job is rejigging the lights in the grow room. Now that the largest plants have been removed, the lights can be lowered and the remaining plants thus require fewer shelves and boards to meet the lights.

This autoflower is the same age as the Tangerine Dreams. But autos like the Pandora develop much more quickly – here with full buds evident before the sativas have even shown initial sex characteristics.

Because the microscope is in hand, I decide to do a quick check on the Pandora. What a comparison! Its trichomes, while present, are uniformly clear and well formed. It is, despite some color change in its bud now, still far away from harvest. Autoflowering strains typically have smaller harvests that mature more quickly. Pandora would seem to be consistent with this: there are numerous colas on this plant but the bud development is pretty sparse at the moment. Hopefully it will thicken in the coming couple of weeks or so until it too is ready for harvest. This plant is about as big as the smallest of the Kushes but its bud development is a couple of weeks ahead of these plants. I'm wondering if, despite its shorter stature, this plant has topped out in terms of vertical growth.

The Deimos seedlings have made their first appearance today. After planting yesterday, they have both already broken the soil. These appear to be geared for fast development.

How to Harvest

1. Use latex gloves. Bud is sticky, sticky, sticky. Touching bud with hands isn't good for bud quality and can lead to smell if you don't wash up after handling plants.

2. Bring drinks and set up music ahead of time so you don't have to take off gloves.

3. Leave adequate time to harvest. Invite a (trusted) helper!

4. Cut at the base of plant with a big cutter. Just above the soil.

5. Cut up the main stem, removing side stems successively. Choose the location for each cut with care, being sure to leave a "hook" on each stem to making hanging/drying easier. Set aside.

6. Once this is all done, take the fan leaves off. Most large ones can be pulled off by hand.

7. If leaves don't come off easily, don't force it – you risk pulling off bud! Cut with scissors when you meet resistance.

8. If you do get loose bud, save it. This can of course still be dried.

9. Trim off smaller leaf matter but be careful not to accidentally trim off bud.

10. Leave smaller sugar leaves that are coated with lots of crystals. These resin-heavy leaves will dry with the bud and provide a good high (they often have high THC content).

11. Hang trimmed stems in a drying room or closet if you have one. You can also string stems to hang between grow rooms if you have a small area between veg and bud rooms (i.e. when a closet or small room has been bisected by polyethylene "walls."

12. Stems that don't have an easy hanger or are too heavy (an excellent problem to have) should be tied to lines using garden ties.

13. When hanging different strains simultaneously, mark off on different rows using tape or other markers.

14. No sampling bud until it is dry and fully cured! No microwaving! (Some guides suggest microwaving as a way of sampling cannabis early. It degrades quality to the extent that it is difficult to judge the bud in any case.)

15. One exception: if using a vaporizer, wet bud can be used in a pinch – for a taste test, for instance. But do this sparingly.

16. Save or dispose of trim. Though its THC content is significantly lower, cannabis trim does contain THC content (typically 5% compared to 15 to 25% for the bud itself). This trim can be prepared to make a marijuana tincture or other edible such as butter or oil. It can even be used dry to make tea (that is admittedly not as tasty as Earl Grey, but which will provide a buzz that the latter does not).

Step-by-Step: Harvesting

1. Plants that dry out before harvest will dry more quickly post-harvest.

2. Cut the main stem at the base using shears.

3. Be careful not to over-handle THC-laden bud. Work gently.

4. Create hooks when cutting off stems to make for easy hanging.

5. Use smaller scissors for trimming fan leaves.

6. Cut stems to a length that your drying area can accommodate.

7. Trim large fan leaves before moving on to a closer trim.

8. Don't cut off resin-coated sugar leaves like these.

9. Trim can be saved for use in teas and tinctures.

10. With large fan leaves removed, time for a closer trim.

11. Dispose of waste frequently – don't track evidence out of your room.

12. A monster terminal cola, thick with bud.

13. Particularly large stems can be divided to make the work easier.

14. Clean scissors regularly with alcohol or trimming will take much longer.

15. Fans without any resin can be discarded.

16. Clean up your work area when finished.

17. Trim drying for later use.

18. A pretty (not so) little row: hang to dry.

Quick and Easy Drying and Curing

1. During drying, plants will create a significant smell. This is most potent for the first couple days. Use air fresheners, incense or other ways to mask smell as needed. Consider this before inviting people who don't know about your garden into the vicinity of your grow area.

2. The drying area should be dark and dry. About 40-50% relative humidity is best – this can be adjusted via use of a (de-)humidifier. Too far outside this range, bud will dry out more quickly or slowly. Slow and steady drying is best.

3. Check bud after two to three days. It can take a week or more for bud to dry sufficiently but rarely less than three days on the de-leafed stems.

4. Test: stems that bend easily are too wet to trim bud into curing bags. Stems that snap are too dry. Stems that splinter without snapping are just right. Good job, Goldilocks!

5. Have paper bags and clean Mason jars with lids at the ready for curing.

6. Don't over handle; resin on bud can be damaged through rough trade!

7. Clip bud carefully into drying bags. Don't put more than an ounce into each bag. You may wish to leave bags open or to close them depending on whether bud is drying/curing too quickly or slowly. On average, after three days of drying bud on the stem, 3-5 days of curing in bags is needed before placing bud into glass jars for storage.

8. Bud will be ready to be placed in Mason jars when the remaining stem is dry and brittle. Remove as much stem as possible before putting in jars.

9. You may need to leave stem on for dense colas, particularly tops of terminal colas.

10. After all bud is harvested, weigh it. You may wish to record this in your grow journal to compare innovations in your gardening methodology. Results at harvest are the best way to judge what works for you (as are a log of "tasting notes"). However, as with all aspects of your daily grow, ensure this information is secure.

11. For two to three weeks post-curing, you must open or "burp" jars every day or two. This allows new air to circulate and reduces the chances of mold developing in bud that has been jarred while still retaining moisture.

12. Note any moisture on lid as this indicates danger of mold development. If there is significant condensation, consider leaving jars open for longer periods every day.

13. Store jars in a cool, dry, and secure location. Do not store cured bud in a freezer (which increases chance of moisture contamination) or in plastic bags. Appropriately cured and stored bud can last and be enjoyed months, even years later.

14. When ready, enjoy!

Another autoflower is taking off: here, a Deimos has begun to develop in its initial vegetative growth spurt.

Saved by timely action: a Master Kush clone taken from the dying mother is taking off.

Day 64

The Deimos plants have defined leaf structures and proper stems now. The Kush clones look good as well. They should be about a week from transplanting. I'm going to be careful to treat these with kid gloves; there's no sense in mucking about with these given the precarious state of health of Mama Kush. The mass death of the leaf canopy seems largely over, though the older leaves continue to die off daily. Thankfully they are being replaced by new growth that appears to be fine. I have no second doubts about retiring this plant from active service. However, I want to keep it as healthy as possible until such time as I have a definite replacement set up and growing well.

Day 65

What a difference a week makes. Though the Mother Tangerine Dream is only that long removed from its sisters, the difference between the plants is now obvious. The two Tangerines in the bud room have definite bud formations. The hairs produced by this strain are a creamy yellow, even compared to the slightly colored Master Kush. The Mother, though it maintains observable sex characteristics (these will slowly decline and

Note the relative light penetration: the vegging plant on the left is too dense for fluorescents to work effectively below the upper canopy. The Pandora shows the effectiveness of a good trim.

disappear over the next week or so), is now outpaced in terms of development. The contrast illustrates how quickly the plants mature in the 12/12 light cycle, even when they're slow pokes like these Tangerines.

The Deimos plants each have four true leaves now. They are super dry so I water them liberally. The leaves have yellowed slightly but the hydration should take care of this; they are too young for nutrients in any case. The bud on the Pandora also continues to change color and there are large bud formations even in the lower parts of the plant. This may be the upside of a shorter plant: the light can penetrate deeper into the center of the plant and reach lower branches. So, despite its diminutive size, it may return a healthy harvest after all. Bud formations on upper colas have begun to grow together now. All plants get water as needed then that's it for today.

Day 66

The Pandora looks good, but holy shit, what an ungodly smell there is today. These really must be moving into the major bloom now, and this is an unfamiliar smell. Initially, I thought a plant was either hitting the lights or, more likely, rotting, when I entered the room. A quick smell test told me this was coming from the Pandora. Yikes. I certainly hope

"Twisted Sisters:" These stems are broken strategically during supercropping, but they will bounce back with more robust growth.

it tastes better than it smells!

All plants save for the Kush clones and Deimos seedlings are fed on the appropriate nutrient schedule today. The Deimos plants are progressing normally. Inside the week they will likely need to be moved away from the lights and the major spurt of vegetative growth will begin. I make a mental note to sex these down the road. Though they won't move into the bud room and have been grown from feminized seeds, males are still a possibility that I need to be on the lookout for.

In the bud room today, except for some minor movement of the lights and spinning of the plants, the major task is to experiment with a technique used to maximize bud production that I have not used to date: super cropping. The goal of super cropping is the same as topping: to increase the quantity of bud produced by manipulating the plants. Super cropping doesn't involve cutting, however. Instead, plants stems are twisted and gently broken: cracked, not snapped apart. If you are too aggressive in your technique you risk destroying one or more otherwise viable stems. The principle here is that stems that have been broken slightly will, after a couple of days for recovery, grow stronger and larger. This results in larger everything – including bud formations. Also, super cropped stems will grow more crooked, assuming the shape that they have been bent into rather than growing straight up into the lights. In retrospect, I've observed that super cropped plants tend to have stems that bow out, sweeping gently out to the side and then rising up. This has two principal benefits.

First, super cropped stems themselves will, when bent sufficiently, allow more direct access of light to calyxes and bud formations all along the stems rather than hitting merely the tops, a situation where the light will be blocked out from lower stems and bud. Though these bowed stems take up more space in the grow room (something that could be an issue in truly cramped quarters), they without a doubt produce more bud – from 30% to as much as 50% more than non-super cropped plants! It is a procedure worth the time and effort to be sure.

Second, and related to this, the bowed stems open up space in the center of the plant. This allows small stems that would otherwise get lost beneath one or more large colas to spurt up and move toward the lights and create their own bud on mini-colas. A good number of these will naturally spring up to fill the void created by the main stems moving out of the way. Indeed, the effect can be a lower, secondary canopy of bud with many small stems, each producing its own nug of bud.

Super cropping is best done towards the very end of vegetative growth. I now do it after topping so that the multiple stems produced can each be bent, sometimes more than once, so that they are trained to allow for maximum bud production. Today, however, I proceed with my maiden effort on the smaller Tangerine #2. This was a conscious calculation, as Tangerine #1 is bigger and looks more likely to produce a nice harvest. Tang #2 was the much smaller plant and was traumatized already. As such, there is less of a risk of losing yield in playing with its development. It hasn't produced clear bud yet anyway, so it should be okay. With luck, the super cropping will spike its development so that it can approach or even catch its sister at harvest.

Day 67

The super cropping appears to have worked well. The two branches I "broke" last night have curled sideways and growth continues. There

Believe it or not: these fan leaves were all taken from the single mother in one go. It is better to act early to keep growth under control if cultivating a mother for long-term use.

are visible signs of a scar on the epidermis of the one stem. Still, the plant looks healthy so I've continued with another three stems today. The plant is left looking pretty broken down now but should be fine.

The Kush clones also look a little worse for wear now. They have yellowed leaves at the bottom. This is normal. The plants are feeding on these leaves as the root structures finish forming in the soil (presumably–I won't know for sure for another few days). The rest of the plants get a liberal watering and we close down shop for the night.

Day 68

Without much else to do, today is mainly a day for Mother maintenance. Mother Kush shed another handful of necrotic leaves tonight, but this is much reduced from when it was replanted. I am now being far pickier, and there is still plenty of green on the leaves I'm taking off. Also, three stems nearing the lights required chopping, which is a definitive sign

A much more trim mother: it may have been too late, but this trim was an attempt to save it before quitting and starting over...

...though the fact that leaves continue to yellow and die is not a good sign.

that the plant still grows! I also chopped away a handful of smaller wispy stems in the lower sections of the plant that were sucking energy but had no serious shot of being useful for cloning.

Mother Tangerine also required topping on another couple of stems today to batten down vertical growth. It is looking really strong. Also note that the white hairs that are evidence of female sex are still present on couple of the cola tops, so it hasn't completely reverted yet. This is important because I don't want to clone this plant until it has completely reverted to its vegetative state.

Day 69

There's not much to do plant-wise in either room today. However, the gnats, which are still largely absent from the bud room, are massing on the Veg side. The traps aren't sufficient. I will treat with the Mosquito Dunk again tomorrow during watering. If this isn't sufficient to tamp

After drying, cure and store bud in glass mason jars. Keep them in a dark place at room temperature. No freezing.

them down, I may have to head back to my local grow store to pursue other potential solutions. I also resolve to do some more reading online for potential cures.

The harvested Kush is now dried and bottled for curing. Each bottle will be "burped" daily. That is, the lid will be removed and checked for any buildup of condensation, which can promote mold. Leaving your lids off daily for 15 or 20 minutes is good practice; it cycles out the air and finishes the bud off. These are now ready to try; vaporizing some, I find that they have a great finish. This is a happy end to this particular crop and each Kush produced around an ounce of bud each.

Because this grow is now in its final stages, much of its story has now been told. A daily recounting of events, most of which are not notable (water/dry, water/dry, feed/dry – repeat, move lights, etc.) has been covered sufficiently. This is, or (hopefully) should be the easiest part of the daily grow. And though it is a daily grow, we can restrict our observations for the most part to noteworthy developments only over the period of a few days at a time.

Now the Tangerines are into full bloom. It is particularly exciting to track the development of strains new to your garden.

Days 70 to 75

Now that things have settled down I take off for the weekend. With my guest gardener taking care of things, the grow is in capable hands. Before I leave I meet briefly with my helper, prepping them for what they need to do. I also leave detailed notes whenever I go away, taking particular care to be specific about feed requirements and watering schedules. Generally speaking, I also move the plants a bit further away from the lights than normal. Of course, this isn't ideal, growthwise, but I also want to keep things as simple as possible for someone who is helping me out. Jigging lights around and/or futzing with shelves can be a serious pain in the ass and is not something to throw to a guest doing you a favor if you can avoid it. I also want to minimize the chance of light burns in case my helper isn't able to check the plants in as timely a manner as I do. It should go without saying but always leave a contact number just in case there are any problems that require your advice.

The plants were fed on Day 73, while I was away. This feed presents

Bud sites are now in full bloom on the Tangerines. Though Indica-dominant cannabis would be nearing harvest, these still have a ways to go.

an example of the necessity of crystal clear instructions: there was a goof and the Pandora got Veg feed initially (which was then topped up with Bud feed once the mistake was caught). Given the unorthodox placement of a budding plant in the veg room, this was an easy confusion. It's my garden, so ultimately it's my fault. Thankfully it shouldn't be a big deal in the grand scheme of the grow.

Tangerine #1 is now the tallest, biggest plant in the bud room, topping 22 inches. Tangerine #2 has fully recovered from the super cropping and is now growing apace, though it's still much shorter at about 18 inches. It's tough to measure this plant actually as the super crop has left it in a wishbone shape with two main stems, which are bowed, and a lower canopy of smaller stems. The Kushes continue to grow vertically too but their stems are starting to grow heavy with bud. They should be two weeks or so from harvest and nearly finished with vertical growth. On schedule, the bud at the cola tops has begun to change color. It seems very clear now that the Tangerine Dream will take several weeks longer. Online reading confirms this: most sativa

The Deimos and Kush clones are developing without incident. Caring for fragile young plants is arguably more important than care for those in bloom in terms of the ongoing viability of your garden. A mistake here can set you back weeks.

plants will take about 25-30% longer to bring to harvest than indica plants. Let's hope they're worth the wait.

We'll have to do a lot less waiting with the Pandora. Its growth appears to be done and the plant has finished at 17 inches in either direction. Its bud is thickening markedly now; it has in one section of the lower branches actually grown together across two stems. For such a small plant, this is shaping up to be a potentially big haul!

The Kush clones and Deimos seedlings are transplanted at this time. The Deimos plants have nice advanced root structures despite their smaller size relative to the clones. The Kush clones had very, very small root growth but it was sufficient for transplantation. They took on the look of a "ball" of root, like an ingrown hair that is about to burst (I hope!).

I haven't taken any further action on the gnats yet but they continue to buzz around. Though the Dunk may have reduced their numbers somewhat, I'm growing tired of their presence and am going to try to wipe them out using any means necessary before this particular grow is done.

Preparing for Leaving Your Garden (Temporarily)

1. Have a close, trusted friend or two upon whom you can depend to care for your garden while you are away. Obviously, it helps if they are sympathetic to or interested in learning about your hobby.

2. For longer absences, meet ahead of time if possible to review instructions.

3. Even if you meet to discuss things, always prepare clear, written instructions with a contact number and leave this in close proximity to the garden.

4. Avoid discussing your garden overtly by phone, text or email. Devise a few easy to remember codes to mask what you are talking about with guest gardeners (Big Brother probably isn't watching, but you never know!).

5. Clearly label all nutrients and detail the appropriate feed schedule.

6. Plan in advance. It is a good idea to have a set of generic instructions ready to go at all times that you can tweak easily if you have to leave in a hurry.

Days 76-80

The seedlings are looking strong and healthy, as is one of the Kush clones. The second is yellowish still and a bit compromised. It appears I have my new Mother, the healthy plant, and can hopefully nurse the other to health so that it can be brought to bud. By Day 80, it is basically out of the woods.

This is the first time in a while that my co-gardener Ms. Woodward has made an appearance. Observing the steadily browning Pandora bud, she opines that it looks ready for harvest. I'm inclined to agree, but I also know that she is excited to try the new strain and that might be making her somewhat biased. Despite the advancing color change in the bud which is observable to the naked eye, the microscope shows that only about a quarter of all trichomes have changed from clear to cloudy and there is little amber coloring at all. Despite what Ms. Woodward says, I think this plant is still a week or more away from harvest.

Bud formations have developed across the upper cola of the Tangerines now. Tangerine #2 required strategic staking: the two major colas were so much taller than the under-canopy that the latter field of bud was being deprived of sufficient proximity to the lights. Therefore, the

Tangerines: bigger by the day. Take care to stake and train marijuana away from lights when needed, particularly tall sativas, which can be tricky to grow in tight spaces.

two main stems have been staked to bring them under the main lights in the bud room, allowing the smaller singles to be dropped to just over top of the canopy. It is an inelegant but effective solution to the problem. The Mothers are both looking good: Tangerine Mother has finally dropped any pretense of flowering. It is now ready for cloning. The Kush Mother has really thinned out but has several stems that look like they will be salvageable for cloning. This is my sole goal with this plant now: to coax it through to a point when the best possible clones can be taken, then take it out of service.

The big effort during this stretch was to treat the soil to eliminate the gnats. The suggested treatment at my grow store was Neem oil, a natural additive thought to make soil inhospitable to many insects. There is a fair amount of online debate about whether Neem oil or Mosquito Dunk is the superior treatment. Despite there being adherents to both camps, I've decided to use both since both treatments are organic and largely benign in terms of plant development.

I follow the instructions and mix the oil with water and dish soap, then water the plants. The Dunk is broken up into water and this is added as well. These treatments target the larvae and homes of the emerging gnat populations and are to be applied monthly. To combat the existing gnats,

Step-by-Step: Guide to Neem Oil and Mosquito Dunk

1. *Measure out Neem oil into water. Be sure not to splash onto leaves to avoid burns.*

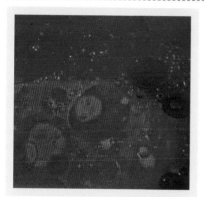

2. *Mix as well as possible – though the oil will stand out in the water.*

3. *Better to have dunk and other pest remedies on hand in advance.*

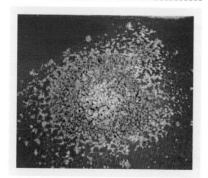

4. *Measure out into water. Do this separately from oil or nutrients.*

5. *Trim affected leaves to more easily measure the progress of remedies.*

Staking/Training Plants

1. Plants that have a solid root base will rarely have to be staked until well into development of heavy bud.

2. Metal garden stakes are superior to bamboo or other stakes (the latter can leak dye into soil and are more likely to attract contaminants).

3. Plastic ties (for water resistance) are best for tying plants to stakes. Be sure to leave room for plant growth. Ties should be used more as a sling than a noose!

4. As plants move into the latter stages of budding, stems will naturally sag under the weight of the bud. Stake plants, repeatedly if necessary, to maintain proximity to lights and to avoid plants falling into each other.

5. Plants, particularly Sativa strains that tend to be taller, may be trained down to reduce vertical growth and keep plants under lights.

6. Ensure that stakes do not butt up against lights or other equipment. Safety first!

I have purchased an insecticide that is billed as organic and derived from chrysanthemums. As it came from my local grow store and I've discussed its use with the staff, I am confident that it can be used safely. It can be sprayed three times, once every five days. Still, when spraying the soil tops, I wrap the bottom of each plant in a tea towel to shield them from as much exposure as possible. Moreover I wouldn't apply this spray, however billed, to plants that are close to harvest. This spray is said to be safe for application on plants meant for consumption. Still, these will need extra care to ensure that they are well and truly flushed before harvest.

The post-mortem on these interventions is largely positive. By Day 80, the number of gnats is much reduced. There are few actively flying around, though they still fly out from under the pots when disturbed. Still, at the very worst I've tamped back their development to a more manageable level. Hopefully they can be wiped totally in the coming weeks. The only drawback is that a number of leaves have been burnt through inadvertent splashes with Neem-laden water. An important note here: avoid splashing Neem oil mixture on leaves as it leaves a sticky residue that burns lightly. Plants won't be compromised fundamentally, but the close proximity of the plants to the T5s burns the residue. This is most serious for the seedlings. Had I known this, I would have poured with more care. Take your time with this should you use Neem on your plants.

Days 81-85

The Kushes have now finished their vertical growth, topping out at 20 to 22 inches tall each. They have clear crystallization now and are already more brown than the two Kushes in the previous harvest. Though I had initially estimated an extended grow time, these could be ready as early as next week.

Tangerine #1 is now over two feet tall and Tangerine #2 has caught the Kushes, though this is a bit deceptive; only the two main colas are this high. The lower canopy is only a little over 14 inches tall. Bud production has now started to build on these as well. They will still be substantially longer to harvest as there is no color change and the bud is still relatively early in its development. These plants, though they've taken extra time and were initially fussier than the Master Kushes to grow, are really magnificent; they are thick bushes with lots of cola/bud development. I'm excited to see how the first harvest compares and

The first of the bud formations have begun.

And now they begin to form a continuous line of bud linking calyxes.

These sativa-dominant hybrids are much taller than their indica cousins.
Careful planning is needed when growing indoors.

The excitement is in the budding, but the next crop-to-be is where the work
– and your attention – is best directed to maintain a continuous crop cycle.

These two Tangerines are the same age, but the one on the left is well into budding. The one on the right has been successfully returned to vegetative growth and has assumed the role of Mother.

am bearing in mind that the first harvest from seed will often have slightly skewed timelines. I wouldn't be surprised if the first batch of Tangerine Dream clones matures at a substantially quicker rate.

The babies (Deimos seedlings and Kush clones) continue to develop well. Over a few days they recover from the Neem burns. They need to be moved away from the lights every couple of days now.

I treat the soil for a second time with the insecticide spray, leaving out the Pandora, which is now ready to harvest – it gets two flushes over a few days to thoroughly clean its soil. Although the number of gnats is very small, I'm hoping this will be the knockout punch. To that end, I use a screwdriver to agitate the soil, stirring up the top inch to disrupt the breeding ground of gnats. I have still yet to see larvae though so I am getting hopeful that this cocktail of Dunk/Neem/spray has knocked the gnats out. Stirring up the soil isn't a bad thing in any case, as it's good to keep things fresh for the plants rather than letting a hard pan of soil develop.

Be sure to "burp" jars when curing to remove any residual moisture. If you do not, you risk mold developing.

Days 86-90

Day 86 is harvest day for the Pandora. It is quicker than the non-auto-flowering plants, though not incredibly so. Rather than taking the whole plant down at the root, I decided as an experiment to take each stem off about a third of the way up from its base. This will give the lower half of the plant somewhere from a day to a week to ripen further (bud on lower branches is almost always smaller and less ripened due to its distance from the lights). I end up harvesting the rest of the plant on Day 89, and find that the buds are barely if at all increased in size. They are browner and riper, however, so this wasn't a total waste. The final haul is what is most encouraging: my largest yet, just shy of two ounces from this plant. After trimming the stems and moving the Pandora bud to the curing stage, the first samples are available for testing. It vaporizes with a slightly lemon taste with a definite pine undertone. Don't be surprised if you begin to approach your harvests of different strains much like a sommelier would approach different bottlings of wine. This is another aspect of a rewarding hobby.

The Kushes and the Tangerines continue to be watered and fed on their normal schedule. I'm a little concerned that it appears that these Kushes will be smaller again than my last crop, which had been my

Step-by-Step: Harvesting Pandora

1. *Cut the main stem at the base. Remember to remove all telltale signs of cannabis when disposing of soil.*

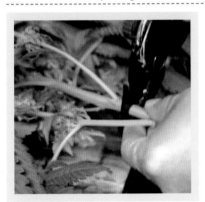 

2. *Cut strategically: make hooks for ease in hanging to dry. Clothespins or twist ties also work to hang stems without hooks.*

3. *If harvesting more than one strain simultaneously, be sure to keep plants separate when trimming and hanging.*

4. *Trim away fan leaves. Be careful not to pull bud off with the trim.*

5. *Wear gloves to avoid over-handling the bud.*

6. *Clean scissors frequently to remove sticky resin and speed up trimming.*

7. *Set aside trimmed bud.*

8. Hang to dry. Be sure to check daily so that they are not left to dry too long.

9. Weigh dried bud when bottling and track your yields to improve your practice.

Even a small space can be maximized if used wisely and with planning.
Here, three sets of vegetating plants use the same space.

shortest to date. This isn't a total surprise given the challenges we've encountered on this grow: a gnat infestation and the attendant treatments as well as colder than expected temperatures as a result of the venting fan debacle. I will keep detailed notes to see what effect, if any, these developments have on the harvest.

Speaking of the harvest, the Kush should be ready in a week or less according to the calendar. Still, as of Day 87, less than a quarter of the trichomes have ripened sufficiently. These may take a bit longer to reach harvest. The one nice development in here is the fact that Kush #3, which had such a traumatic time while vegging, has an inordinate number of thick bud developments in its lower branches. This may be a result of the response to the trauma. It could also, like the Pandora, be a case of smaller plants developing more bud than taller ones because more bud has a chance to fully develop in closer proximity to the lights. This is something I will continue to monitor, measure, and experiment with far beyond this grow. It may ultimately lead me to aim for shorter plants if that means bigger yields.

Day 89 saw the retirement of the Kush Mother. I am confident now

Sometimes less is more: two plants with more space and light penetration might yield almost as much bud as these three Tangs rammed together will.

that one Kush clone (at least) is healthy enough to replace it. As a result of removing this gargantuan plant, and the departed Pandora, I engage in a significant rejig of the shelves in the veg room. The lights are dropped almost a foot, which makes maintenance of this room much easier all round. The first clones are also taken from the Tangerine Mother at this time. This is the first go around with these so I will proceed with caution and see how they respond.

One of the Deimos plants has taken off. The growth is explosive now. It needs to be moved away from the lights daily and requires a doubling down on nutes. Its leaves began to yellow until I bumped up its feed schedule. You'll learn to trust your gut in these situations, but the ability to do so comes from vigilance and review. I think this is just an outlier plant, a real monster, as opposed to the second Deimos or the Kush clones being weak. This isn't totally abnormal: many strains at the F1 stage have multiple phenotypes, and some are faster and bigger than others. In addition, the first generation of any hybrid benefits from explosive growth due to a genetic phenomenon known as "hybrid vigor." Regardless, seeds are unlike clones that come from a single source, the Mother.

The Deimos (pictured on the right) is almost into full maturity (and eventual budding) even though it is small. Despite smaller yields and the necessity of constant germination, autos are a great solution to the problem of a truly tiny grow area.

To maximize yields, it is essential to compare and chart differences across plants in the same strain. Propagate the healthiest, largest specimens to make your garden as healthy and efficient as possible.

Seeds contain genetic variations and will come with larger and smaller results depending on the various phenotypes and their vigor. Regardless of your own efforts, some plants will be a bit different. This is why growing multiple seeds is important before starting a Mother plant; you will want to have several to choose from so that you can select the hardiest and most appropriate plant for the specifics of your needs and grow situation.

The gnats continue to be a work in progress. There aren't many of them, but they are still here. Grrrr.

Sun	Mon	Tue	Wed	Thurs	Fri	Sat
				61	62	
64		66	67	68		70
71	72	73	74	75	76	77
78		80	81	82	83	84
85	86	87		89	90	

Month three: Most indica strains will have been harvested by now. After week twelve, remaining time is devoted to the maturation of sativa strains.

Days 91-95

The first part of this grow ends over these next few days. The three Kushes are flushed and harvested on Day 92. As with the Pandora, I leave the lowest branches of the Kushes intact and return them to the bud room to ripen up. They respond quickly, not growing in size but browning significantly within a couple of days and producing noticeable amounts of crystalizing resin. By Day 95 the main stems are trimmed and cured. These were definitely shorter than in my previous Kush grows. Still, the longest are over a foot long and quite thick. The largest turns out to be Kush #3, the plant that had the hardest time developmentally.

One security concern of a minor but notable variety: I mentioned in passing to my co-grower early on Day 95 that I would be bottling the harvest that night. Excited, she took matters into her own hands, literally, while I was out during the day. No big deal, right? Wrong. I had been careful to hang the stems from the three plants separately from one another to measure the harvest of each plant accurately. Then she had at them, not knowing that I wanted separate counts. In fairness,

Step-by-Step: Kush Harvest Day 92

1. Prep your work area.

2. Cut individual stems.

3. Trim the non-bud mass out.

4. Thin it down to colas. Remove all fan leaves.

5. Measuring colas is useful, both to measure harvest and ensure there is sufficient space to hang them.

6. Take in your harvest. This Master Kush has paid off nicely.

Success! These Kush clones have responded to the trauma of topping with vigorous new growth.

it's all going to the same place. But it's a reminder, however small and harmless, that security is an issue, even with those you trust. In any case, the three plants averaged just about bang on one ounce each. This is hardly my largest harvest (the two Kushes in the very next grow topped out at a bit less than one and a half and just shy of two ounces respectively), but a good one. Any time I hit an ounce per plant, I'm happy. My fluorescent system is cheap and easily provides enough cannabis for my needs.

In the veg room, I super crop the two Kushes. This explains the large harvest mentioned above; I am a convert to the church of the super crop. One little blip: I am a bit rough when bending one stem, and it snaps a bit too far. Though I give it a chance to right itself overnight, hoping it will re-cover, it ultimately dies. This will amount to a topping in the grand scheme of things so no big deal. However, with practice I establish a habit of not so much bending the stems as lightly crushing them (I know, a "light" crush sounds like an oxymoron) until they make a slight crunching sound. When bending, I also take care to place a finger on the stems, around which I

Step-by-Step: Harvesting of Lower Branches

Having left the lower branches to ripen under the lights for a few more days, I now am able to harvest those lower branches for some more bud.

1. Check trichomes daily until ready to harvest.

2. Cut main stems to clear pots.

3. Remove any large fan leaves by hand.

4. Trim smaller leaves as needed.

5. Remove remaining trim.

6. Prepare trimmed bud to hang to dry.

It is normal for new clones to cannibalize their own fan leaves while roots develop. Be sure to cut them tall enough that they have leaves that can be spent.

bend them; the absence of this finger is the surest way to inadvertently snap a stem. Also, one thing you can try is this: in the case of a snapped stem, stake the affected stem, being sure to tie the severed stem sections together closely. In most cases, they will heal back together.

Kush #2 develops some strange rounded leaves in a ball formation in the center of the plant. These leaves are deformed and definitely lack a cannabis shape in any case. Instead, they look more like the fetal leaves but larger. After giving this ball formation a few days, I cut it back. This just didn't look right and given that this plant still has a good amount of time to veg, it should recover and this will amount merely to an early topping.

The Deimos plants are transplanted into the largest pots and topped. Deimos #1 grows unbelievably quickly. It hits the lights not once, not twice, but three times – and this is even with several moves away from the lights. Deimos #2 is as wide and thick as its cohort is thin. Oddly, it has taken on a similar shape to Tangerine #2 in the bud room: two taller stems in a pitchfork like formation with a lower shelf of growth. Both

Now this looks more like a citrus-inspired strain: bud has begun to turn from white to orange as these Tangerines move closer to harvest. Noting such differences across strains are a great part of this hobby.

sprout numerous white hairs at the calyxes. They are sexed and close to bud development, a day short of a month from putting the seeds in soil. These will have the advantage over the departed Pandora of being treated like an autoflowering plant actually should be: they will stay in the 18/6 light cycle to harvest.

The clones all develop without incident. This wouldn't be worth noting except for the fact that the Kushes were taken from the dying Mother and their health was very much in doubt. The Tangerines are the first batch of clones and you never know exactly what you're going to get on your first new grow of anything. All are doing well, developing normally with occasional spritzing, the warmth and humidity of the bubble and occasional yellowed leaves as their roots develop.

In the bud room, only the two Tangerine Dreams remain, with their vertical growth apparently done and their bud production increasing at a nice pace now. I would estimate that these will be another couple of weeks at least to maturity as only the very first bit of bud has changed color and it is still gaining mass.

These clones could be identified as a sativa-dominant strain simply by looking at the long, slender fan leaves – but labeling is still a must to maintain an organized garden.

Days 96-100

On Day 96 the gnats are crazy: it is the first time they've actually buzzed me directly. What the heck? I sprayed the gnats themselves, around the pots and in the bottom/soil of anything not near harvest. I hope that this is the death throes. If not, I'm going to have to go nuclear in terms of my treatments, because this is no good.

By the next day, the gnats have settled back down.

The tall Deimos is growing well; so tall, in fact, that I would think it was stretched if I hadn't been on top of keeping it close to the lights, (too close, actually, given the repeated burns). This height requires that the Tangerine Dream Mother be raised closer to the lights as well as being topped regularly. This allows the Deimos to max out while avoiding the excessive height problem encountered by the now retired Mother Kush. Deimos #1 hits 17 inches, 14 after the interventions, while its sister is only six high. It also slows them down temporarily when they are topped and super cropped, in that order. Logically, it is best to follow this order of intervention rather than the reverse, if only because

The terminal colas on these Tangerines have begun to thicken and grow heavy. Staking such stems is often a must to keep plants upright.

Super cropping, before and after. Proceed with care and the result can be more bush-like plants that increase yields by allowing stems more even access to light.

topping first allows for additional stems to super crop later. By Day 100, Deimos #1 needs three stakes to survive in the cramped grow conditions and to support the extensive stems.

The feeding of the Tangerines in the bud room spikes now as their bud development takes off. The flowers are thickening and filling in up and down the stems. The two plants have topped out at 25 and 23 inches and are nearly 22 inches across. The "shelf" on Tangerine #2 stands 16 inches high and is growing increasingly thick, taking on an almost lawn-like consistency.

Days 101-105

By Day 101 the bud on the Tangerines emits a tasty odor when touched. They really do have an unmistakably orange scent. This is noted when the bud is handled with the microscope. On check, the trichomes show some initial change from clear to cloudy, which denotes the coming fullness of maturity. Unlike the Kushes, the bud on these is browning from the bottom up. This isn't even necessarily strain specific. This can vary from grow to grow, even within the same strain, from the same Mother. The Tangerines also slowly begin to drop necrotic leaves that mark the normal approach of readiness for harvest. However, they are still a week away or more.

The Kushes join the Tangerines in the grow room, a few days apart. This move is made as much because I'm out of space in the veg room given the explosion of the Deimos plants as the Kushes being ready for prime time. Still, they're looking good to go. I'm rewarded for the timely move: the Kushes literally pop at the calyxes within a couple days of moving to the bud room.

The clones are transplanted at this time. The Tangerines have healthy root development, but the Kushes have less so. This isn't entirely surprising and is likely a product of having been taken from a Mother in steep decline. Still, they seem to have enough roots formed to have made transplantation okay. The Deimos plants also continue to clip along in terms of vertical growth, both with clearly defined bud formations now, growing bigger daily.

Carelessly, I lose the tallest top cola on Deimos #1. First it hits the light

This is what you are working for. Sweet!

Successfully cloned, a developing root ball is evident here.

Watch for new growth to determine when clones are ready for transplantation to pots and a regular feeding schedule.

Talk about phenotype variation: this Deimos is tall and stringy, despite being kept as close to the light as its more diminutive sister.

Step-by-Step: Automated Hydro Cloning

1. *Prep all materials – don't mix whisky and water!*

2. *Trim clones to an appropriate length.*

3. *Coat liberally with rooting gel.*

4. *Ensure that clones are seated stably in pods.*

5. *Place pods in cloning machine. Ensure that water stays cool.*

6. *Continue to spritz leaves until roots begin to form.*

Whoops! This tallest cola has been burnt to a crisp. The plant is ultimately okay, but check frequently when a growth spurt is underway.

That's more like it: kept a safe distance from lights, a nice healthy bud forms here.

and is burnt. Then, when attempting to train it away from the lights with stake and ties, I snap it off. Damn. Still, there's lots and lots of dispersed bud on this plant. This was early enough in the budding process that this should come out in the wash. It may be moot in any case: the lights have been moved nearly to their uppermost extent so I'm basically out of room in both directions now. The shelves holding the Tangerine Mother and babies continue to be raised to keep pace with this giraffe of a plant.

Kush #2 lags a bit behind its sister and needs an extra week or so of vegging. It had the excised leaf ball. A leaf ball trim should be approached and followed with care. It will be ready for transfer to the bud room shortly in any case.

Days 106-110

When "traditional medicine" doesn't work, look for the alternatives. The gnats are the disease, and I am getting sick of them. My next attempts at a cure involve raw potato wedges and cinnamon dusting the surface of the pots' agitated soil. The idea behind each is somewhat

Potato slices and cinnamon: it is worth experimenting with home remedies for pest treatment – they are organic and cheap. Potato slices are said to attract pest larvae.

I can't say I had definitive success with these home cures, but the problem did clear up shortly after I employed them. Either way, the impact on the plants was nil, which is the whole point.

different but complementary.

The slices of potato are placed around the stems. They are meant to be magnets for gnat larvae. The cinnamon targets the real root of the problem, pun intended; they deal with the fungus affecting the roots rather than the gnats themselves. The idea here is to deprive the pests of their food. Its application does bother them, however, and they jump from the soil when it is applied.

Within five days the gnats are much reduced. There are many dead on top of the lights and in any water remaining in the pans. The potatoes

Even training can't keep this Tang stem under the lights.

Main buds have begun to brown properly now, signaling approaching harvest.

don't attract any larvae, at least nothing visible. Moreover, they shrivel and begin to decompose within a couple of days and need to be thrown out. A second application to agitated soil on Day 109, coupled with reduced watering (reduced so much that the Tangerine Mother is drooping by the time it is fed on Day 110), seems to do the trick. Still, the gnats have been beaten back again but are not reduced to zero.

The Tangerines continue to mature. By the book, they will be ready for harvest on Day 115: four months from seed, almost to the day. Crystals are spread thick across the tops of both plants. Multiple dying leaves in the lower sections of each plant indicate that the plants are nearly ready for harvest. A microscope check confirms this. The trichomes are cloudy with some withering but they are still at least a week away. They are given their last feed on the Ripen schedule and I settle in for the last days of this grow.

The Deimos plants have (thankfully) stopped growing, as Deimos #1 was nearly out of room at almost 26 inches tall. Each has started to bud significantly. Like the Kushes coming to bud in the other room, they are moving into full maturity and have been switched to Bloom feed. The

Using a cloning machine can take a bit of practice and "trial and error" to master. But, when successful, the result is new root growth and the possibility of mass-producing your garden's next generation of marijuana.

super crop of each plant has created lots of bud with good light exposure up and down the bowed stems. I accentuate this by cutting a few big fan leaves out of the center of each plant to facilitate the growth of several smaller stems up closer to the lights. One smaller stem is staked to move closer to the lights as well. All are on track for what looks to be a solid harvest – but that is a story for another grow.

Days 111-115

On Day 112, in an attempt to ensure that the mistakes that led to "nute lock' on the last Kush Mother are not repeated, the Tangerine Dream Mother's soil is flushed. It responds well. The leaf canopy is green and healthy with no signs of leaf burns caused by salt build-up in the pots. The vegging Kush is developing into a more than adequate replacement for the Master Kush Mother. From here, I'll move to a balanced cloning schedule of Kush and Tangerines: two at a time along with a couple of autoflowering strains from seed. The space in both grow rooms is being used at maximum efficiency and is producing a minimum of five ounces of bone dry, de-stemmed, and meticulously trimmed bud every six weeks. This harvest bears the quality of a product developed with the care that only a home grow allows. It is less contaminated, has fewer stem fragments, and has fewer leaves crammed in with the flowers than cannabis purchased from a street dealer, or from a commercial medical marijuana provider. Buying from a dealer often leads to wet, badly trimmed bud. Home-grown cannabis is always better because you know exactly what went into the plant and how it was grown and cured, and how it should be smoked (or vaped, or cooked with, etc.). The bud is cured to enhance taste. All this TLC equals lots of THC. It is not only a relaxing and engaging hobby, but

A new Mother begins to take shape.   *Needs a trim, but this new Mother is a more manageable height.*

Hedge your bets: while experimenting with a cloning machine for the first time, keep a second set of clones using proven methods. This makes experimentation interesting but low-stakes.

Step-by-Step: Tang Harvest

1. *Oh sativa – worth the extra wait.*

2. *Cut down plants.*

3. *Separate stems.*

4. *Remove fan leaves.*

5. *Trim bud down as much as is possible.*

6. *Hang completed stems until ready for ready for curing.*

Sun	Mon	Tue	Wed	Thurs	Fri	Sat
						91
92		94		96	97	
99	100	101	102	103		105
106	107		109	110	111	112
113		115				

The final countdown: one aspect of growing under T5 fluorescents to keep in mind is that grow times can stretch a bit as seed company estimates are often based on use of more powerful bulbs. This last three weeks sees the conclusion of the Tangerines and the next round of Master Kush is only days away.

also a productive and highly (pardon the pun) satisfying enterprise.

In the bud room, the smell is fairly overwhelming just prior to harvest, even with the exhaust fan running continuously. Because the fan is operating properly (now), the smell can only be detected when the room's tarp is opened. Otherwise, the smell is undetectable more than ten feet from the grow rooms. After a final check with the microscope, the Tangerines are harvested on Day 115. Unlike the last batch of Kushes, they produce bud in smaller, separated nugs rather than one continuous formation along the stems. These smaller formations are, however, far more numerous. After three days of drying, they are trimmed and bottled. It is a successful haul: nearly three ounces of dried bud. It smells like citrus and even tastes like a Creamsicle, at least straight away. This is reduced with curing. It is without a doubt the most potent bud I have produced to date. It is mind-blowingly good.

Postscript

The Deimos plants come to harvest a few weeks after the conclusion of this grow diary. Their bud, while less impressive, is still plentiful (in excess of an ounce per plant) and potent, if not "over the moon" strong as its name would indicate. The Kush batch that was just beginning to bloom at this time comes to harvest six weeks later. These, the first Kushes I had super cropped, topped out at better than an ounce and a half each, which is by far the largest harvest of this strain to date. That is definitely my takeaway tip from this grow: call me the super crop convert. It is a great way to increase yield.

The gnat problem was finally brought under control, less as a direct result of any of the interventions, and more by accident: while away, the guest gardener allowed the plants to dry out much longer than I typically do. It was only an extra night, but by the time I returned, the Tangerine Mother in particular was a saggy, droopy mess. Though I was initially concerned that the lack of water had fundamentally compromised the plant, it came around overnight with ample watering. The unexpected upshot was that the gnats' home was dried out sufficiently that they died off.

Tangerine coloring advances on the bud, finally making the name more than just a clever handle.

Still, the top of the terminal cola remains white. Stay patient, and check with your magnifier if in doubt. Properly matured bud is worth the wait.

My first Tangerine harvest. Not a dream maybe, but not a nightmare either. The first taste is only a few weeks away, leaving time for drying and proper curing.

Or mostly so: the odd one continues to fly around, several months later. But they no longer afflict the garden as they did during this grow.

That is one great aspect of developing your own daily grow: it allows you to experiment, test, and figure out with what is best for your needs. This goes for gardening techniques as well as the harvested bud itself. A home garden is, after initial set up costs, relatively cheap, safe, and secure to run, particularly if you opt for T5 fluorescent lights instead of the hot, expensive, and tougher-to-hide bulbs of professional grows and even most home grows of the past. Gardening is a skill that develops quickly if you are motivated to learn and experiment.

Thank you reader, for joining me on my daily grow. Hopefully you are now better prepared to answer the mundane day-to-day questions that more experienced growers neglect to consider and to deal effectively with the curveballs that will get thrown your way. I wish you the best in your gardening. Happy (daily) grow!

Acknowledgments

If one is lucky, writing a book will be a labor of love - but it is also invariably a great deal of work. The challenge is that much bigger when one is not only writing but also shooting photographs to include in the book. If a writer is very fortunate, they will have a small team of people working on their behalf to smooth out errors, coach and cheerlead said author along as the project moves from a rough hypothetical, to tentative project, to fully formed book. In the Green Candy Press team, I have enjoyed exactly this kind of support. Thank you all.

On a non-technical front, my home garden (or at least an active social life, largely unaffected by the sometimes inconvenient responsibility of tending to the garden) would not be possible without the continued assistance of my good friend and frequent guest gardener Kris. Immense thanks for all that you do to help keep things going, and for your curiosity about and love for horticulture that surely exceeds my own. I hope that we will continue to grow together for years to come.

To my partner, without whom literally none of this would have transpired: what an intriguing and surprising journey this continues to be. I surely wouldn't have guessed at this particular bend in our path together. This avocation (avocations really) would literally have never even occurred to me without you. I am grateful that I could build this for you. I appreciate your patience for the hours I spent locked away in my secret garden, and of course for your support, intelligent feedback and good humor (or at least patience) when I frequently gush about the more mundane aspects of cultivation.

Finally, a big shout out to all of those in government, media, and law enforcement who have and continue to work so hard to perpetuate myths about cannabis in general and the trumped up dangers of home cultivation in particular. More than anything else, your allergy to rational arguments, ongoing resistance to empirical evidence and willingness to pursue costly, unhealthy, illogical and mean spirited prohibition in the face of mounting public opposition to the criminalization of marijuana continues to impress. It is a testament to your collective cynicism and superstition. Without so many of you, I really wouldn't be doing this work at all. You are my primary motivation to teach and support others to grow cannabis for themselves, safely and free from the interference of various groups who share a vested interest in maintaining a monstrously wasteful and wrong-headed status quo. Enjoy your remaining moments being on the wrong side of history, boneheads!